AN INWARD SUN
THE WORLD OF JANET FRAME

I'm not sure that I see life . . . What I see is life *within*. Part of myself is given the menial task of absorbing things . . . I don't know what these things are until I see them in an imaginative light, which is a bright light, without shade — a kind of inward sun.

JANET FRAME, NEW ZEALAND NATIONAL RADIO, MAY, 1970

AN INWARD SUN
THE WORLD OF JANET FRAME

MICHAEL KING
WITH CONTEMPORARY PHOTOGRAPHS BY REG GRAHAM

PENGUIN BOOKS

For June Gordon
who had the idea

PENGUIN BOOKS

Penguin Books (NZ) Ltd, cnr Airborne and Rosedale Roads, Albany,
Auckland 1310, New Zealand
Penguin Books Ltd, 80 Strand, London, WC2R 0RL, England
Penguin Putnam Inc, 375 Hudson Street, New York, NY 10014, United States
Penguin Books Australia Ltd, 250 Camberwell Road, Camberwell,
Victoria 3124, Australia
Penguin Books Canada Ltd, 10 Alcorn Avenue, Toronto,
Ontario, Canada M4V 3B2
Penguin Books (South Africa) (Pty) Ltd, 24 Sturdee Avenue, Rosebank,
Johannesburg 2196, South Africa
Penguin Books India (P) Ltd, 11, Community Centre, Panchsheel Park,
New Delhi 110 017, India
Penguin Books Ltd, Registered Offices: Harmondsworth, Middlesex, England

First published by Penguin Books (NZ) Ltd, 2002

1 3 5 7 9 10 8 6 4 2

Copyright © Michael King, 2002

The image on page 8 is taken from *An Angel at My Table*, © Bridget Ikin.

Designed by Athena Sommerfeld
Typesetting and page layout by Amy Tansell
Printed in Hong Kong by Condor Production Ltd

ISBN 0 14 301838 8
www.penguin.co.nz

CONTENTS

INTRODUCTION

This book, a 'shorter Janet Frame', as one wag said to me, could be considered a more accessible companion volume to *Wrestling with the Angel*, my full-length biography of the writer. It had its genesis in an exhibition I curated for the National Library of New Zealand. That collection of photographs, manuscripts and memorabilia opened in Wellington in 2000 and went on display in Oamaru and Dunedin the following year.

Viewing the Dunedin exhibition in the Hocken Library, Janet Frame's sister June Gordon said to me, 'What a good book this would make.' That prompt, followed by discussions with Janet Frame and members of her extended family, led to production and publication of this book, *An Inward Sun: the World of Janet Frame*.

Like the exhibition of the same name, the book explores some of the textures of Frame's life and the formative episodes that shaped her as a writer of genius: the material poverty of her childhood, the deaths of two sisters by drowning, her incarceration in mental hospitals, her enduring sense of being an outsider. It reveals that her writing is both a response to the deepest existential dilemmas posed by life and a way through and out of those dilemmas.

The 'inward sun' is Frame's own chosen

metaphor for the power of the human imagination. She believes it plays a redemptive role in life, giving meaning to chaos and reasons to continue living in the face of chaos. Her bleakest fictional characters are those for whom the imagination plays no role at all, whose 'inward sun' has gone out or never been ignited.

Just as Janet Frame herself has been pushed to the limits by life's treatment of her, so her 'inward sun' has allowed her to push experience, language and meaning to the limit in an effort to convey nuances that have largely eluded other writers. Few artists anywhere have managed to live and to survive on such a fine creative edge.

For assistance with the preparation of this book I thank Janet Frame, June and Wilson Gordon, Pamela Gordon, Reg Graham and Peter Ireland of the National Library of New Zealand. I acknowledge earlier use of the book's title by Patrick Evans, Elizabeth Alley and the National Library. I am especially grateful to Janet Frame for permission to publish material for which she holds copyright, along with so many photographs from her own collection. I also thank Reg Graham for the use of his recent photographs of Janet Frame and photographs of some of the objects displayed in the National Library exhibition. And I thank the Alexander Turnbull, Hocken and University of Auckland Libraries, the North Otago and Canterbury Museums, Pegasus Press and the *Oamaru Mail* for permission to publish material from their collections.

Others who have kindly provided photographs for reproduction in this book are: Jerry Bauer, Gene Beach, Carl Brandt, George Braziller, Christine Cole Catley, Ann Cawley, Ruth Dallas, Barbara Duggan, Marti Friedlander, June Gordon, Pamela Gordon, Gil Hanly, Bridget Ikin, Kevin Ireland, Gregor Macaulay, James Marquand, John Money, Wendy Patterson, Tom Scott, John Scrivener, Jeffrey Simmons, C. K. Stead and the late May Williamson.

The sources for quotations published in this book can be found in *Wrestling with the Angel*.

MICHAEL KING

CHAPTER ONE KINGDOM BY THE SEA

I wanted an imagination that would inhabit a world of fact, descend like a shining light upon the ordinary life of Eden Street . . . I wanted the light to shine upon the pigeons of Glen Street, the plum trees in our garden, the two japonica bushes . . . our pine plantations and gully, our summer house, our lives, and our home, the world of Oamaru, the kingdom by the sea.

(JANET FRAME: TO THE IS-LAND)

This earliest known photograph of Janet Frame's Scottish-born grandparents, Mary Frame and her blacksmith husband Alex, shows them in front of the house they rented in Hanover Street, Dunedin, in about 1901. The child is their youngest son, Charlie.

JANET FRAME

PART OF THE OPENING SEQUENCE OF JANE Campion's film *An Angel at My Table* shows a small girl with red hair and gumboots crunching her way up a country road towards the viewer. The fields on either side of her are almost unbelievably green. The narrator, in the voice of an adult woman, announces, 'This is the story of my childhood. In August 1924 I was born Janet Paterson Frame. My twin, who was never named, died two weeks later.' This information delivered, the on-screen child, apparently disturbed by contemplation of the lost twin, turns abruptly and runs down the road, away from the viewer.

Thus do history and story and image combine to produce myth. And that image – of the bereft twin with the red, red hair running between fields of green, green grass – has become one that is iconic in and central to New Zealand culture. Like all myths, it is both untrue and true.

The little girl on screen, obviously, is an actress, Alexia Keogh. The bright green fields and clear sky are those of the northern region of the North Island, not the more muted features of Otago and Southland where Janet Frame grew up. And there never was an unnamed twin who died two weeks after Janet Frame was born. There was an embryo twin who passed out of its mother's womb several weeks after conception.

And yet the essence is true. There *was* a small child, who would eventually develop red hair, born in Dunedin in the province of Otago on 28 August 1924. And she *was* called Janet Paterson Frame. As those names might suggest, her father's parents were Lowland Scots who had migrated to New Zealand in the 1870s to escape poverty and unemployment in the Clyde Valley. Paterson was Janet's Scottish grandmother's maiden name. Her mother's family had been predominantly English. Because Janet was brought up in Otago and Southland, which had attracted the bulk of the 68,000 Scots who came to New Zealand in the nineteenth century, it was her father's heritage that left the strongest imprint on her immediate family. As the Frame children grew up, they saw little of their mother's family, the Godfreys, most of whom lived around Picton in the north of the South Island.

Isy and Polly Frame, Janet's aunts, in the second row. JANET FRAME

George Samuel Frame,
Janet Frame's father,
in about 1912, the year
he joined the Railways.
Like his brothers and
sisters, he participated
in the piping, dancing
and recitations spon-
sored by Caledonian
societies throughout
Otago and Southland.
Playing bagpipes was
for many years his
favourite recreation.
JANET FRAME

14

Lottie Clarice Godfrey, the buxom Picton girl two years his senior, whom George Frame married in 1916, one month before he sailed for the battlefronts of France and Belgium.
JANET FRAME

Janet's father, George Samuel Frame, had been born in Oamaru in North Otago. His family shifted to Dunedin when he was five years old. And it was from Dunedin that George and his brothers and sisters participated in the activities of Caledonian Societies, particularly Scottish country dancing and pipe band music. In 1912, when he was eighteen, George joined the Railways Department as a cleaner, with the intention of working his way through the ranks to the position of engine driver.

He was posted to a variety of places in the North and South Islands. By 1914 he was in Picton, where one of his fellow workers introduced him to his sister, Lottie Clarice Godfrey. The Godfreys descended from English gentry and scholars, but had come down in the world since emigrating to New Zealand. Lottie's father Alfred Godfrey was, like George's father, a blacksmith. His family of nine children severely stretched his income and the family were not well off. They were also Christadelphians and opposed the taking up of arms in warfare.

It was probably for this reason that George and Lottie married in secret in Wellington in March 1916. George had already volunteered to join the New Zealand Army as a sapper, to serve in the First World War battlefields in France. Within days of their registry office wedding, George was sailing for Europe on a troop ship. Thus it was that after one week of marriage, George and Lottie were separated for more than three years.

In the course of that separation, George fell in love with an English nurse who was looking after him in an army hospital at Brockenhurst,

George Frame, his lemon-squeezer at a jaunty angle, and the nurse with whom he fell in love while recuperating from pneumonia in Brockenhurst in 1918. Lottie Frame refused his request that he be released from his marriage vows. JANET FRAME

near Southampton. He had been sent there with pneumonia one month before the end of the war. George wrote to Lottie to say that he wished to remain in England and be released from his marriage vows. Lottie declined the request, and George returned to New Zealand in 1919.

In the course of her husband's absence, Lottie had moved to Dunedin to be near George's parents. Once settled there she worked as a domestic servant for Willi and Sara Fels, members of a wealthy Jewish merchant family and grandparents of the future poet and writing patron, Charles Brasch. This was Lottie's second brush with what would come to be seen as a 'literary' family. In Picton she had been similarly employed by Arthur and Mary Beauchamp, grandparents of the writer Katherine Mansfield. Perhaps in part because of these associations, Lottie herself began to write poetry – at first for sheer pleasure, and later as an attempt to earn additional income to help support her young family.

When George Frame returned from Europe in 1919 and rejoined the Railways, he and Lottie were at first estranged, because of the request he had made from Brockenhurst. With the help of the senior Frames they eventually reconciled,

Reunited and fertile after World War One, George and Lottie Frame show off their first-born children, Myrtle and Geordie, at Inchclutha, where Lottie's sister Grace lived on a farm. June Gordon

however, and from the beginning of 1920 they rented a cottage in the Dunedin working-class suburb of St Kilda, close to George's parents. Here they started their own family. Myrtle Joan was born in December 1920; George junior, or 'Geordie', in 1922; another boy, stillborn, in 1924; and Janet, survivor of a pair of twins, in 1924.

George senior was by this time an acting-engine driver. In September 1924, when Janet was less than one month old, he was posted to Outram, seventeen miles south-west of Dunedin. It was here in a railways cottage surrounded by a quarter-acre section that Janet would accumulate her first memories.

Janet Frame outside the house in Richardson Street, Dunedin, where her family lived in 1924, the year she was born.
REG GRAHAM

My mother . . . was big and fat and I poked her fat with my fingers whenever I slept in bed with her. She was warm in bed. I could hear her breathing in and out and every time she moved over I felt to see if she was still there. And then my father would come to bed. He smelt of tobacco that he kept in a brown tin on the mantelpiece. He had striped pyjamas with a tear in the back and he slept near the lamp so he could take charge when the burglars came . . . [We] were very safe, the three of us in bed together.

Other recollections would include the byre with an Ayrshire cow called Betty, an empty kerosine tin which Janet would tow around as her first toy, the birth of her sister Isabel May in 1926, and a walnut tree in the backyard, under which Janet said her first words: 'Pick walnut up, Mummy.' She also remembered

a grey day when I stood by the gate and listened to the wind in the telegraph wires. I looked up and down the white dusty road and saw no one. The wind was blowing from place to place past us, and I was there, in between, listening. I felt a burden of sadness and loneliness as if something had happened or begun and I knew about it . . . In listening to the wind and its sad song, I knew I was listening to a sadness that had no relation to me, which belonged to the world.

Early in 1927 the Frames moved again, this time to the tiny Railways settlement of Glenham, one hundred miles to the south. Here they were largely cut off from other members of the extended Frame family, who had visited frequently in Dunedin and Outram. At Glenham, the immediate family survived the ice and snow of one of the harshest winters ever recorded in Southland. While they waited for a Railways house to become available in neighbouring Wyndham, they lived in three red huts placed on the ground in paddocks opposite the Glenham store.

Late in 1927, in the course of a picnic on the bank of the Mataura River, three-year-old Janet told her brother and older sister what family lore would record as her first story:

Once upon a time there was a birdie. One day a hawt flew out of the sky and ate the birdie (oh poor little birdie). The next day a big bodie came out of the sky and ate up the hawt from eating up the little birdie.

Janet shelters from rain under the walnut tree in Outram where, in 1926, she spoke her first words: 'Pick walnut up, Mummy.' REG GRAHAM

Janet and the Railways house in Wyndham, Southland, to which the Frame family moved from Glenham in 1928. Reg Graham

RIGHT: **Seventy years on, Janet seeks out her old bedroom in the Wyndham house.** Reg Graham

Lottie Frame in the backyard at Wyndham, 1929, with her youngest daughter June, Beauty the house cow and Pansy the calf. JANET FRAME

In 1928 the Frames moved temporarily to Edendale, a dairy factory town; and then on to Wyndham. And it was in Wyndham that Janet began to accumulate in earnest what she would refer to later as her 'remembered life'.

The family's Wyndham home was another Railways house, this time a full-sized one, which sat on the railway line end of Ferry Street on the edge of town. Here they kept another house cow, Beauty, and a calf called Pansy; and a dozen White Leghorn hens and a rooster, with a fowlhouse alongside the vegetable garden. At night, George Frame would walk around the outside of the house playing his bagpipes, piping his children to sleep as he had done in Glenham. Here too Janet's mother began to publish verses each week in the *Wyndham Farmer*, and to be known as 'Lottie C. Frame, local poet'. The youngest member of the family, June, was born in June 1928.

Janet's other important memories from her Wyndham years included Sunday afternoons around the kitchen table, when Lottie attempted to teach her children Bible stories and fundamental Christadelphian beliefs (such as the fact that the unemployed men who began coming to the door as the Great Depression intensified, asking for work and food, might turn out to be angels in disguise); her first visit to a dentist, which so terrified her that she was unwilling to go again until well into adulthood; and her first year at school.

In the course of that year in the primary department of Wyndham District High School Janet experienced what she would later refer to as one of the most troubling episodes of her childhood. The infant teacher, Miss Ethel Botting, made Janet stand in front of the class for almost a whole day after she had taken money from her father's trouser pocket and bought chewing gum for herself and classmates. She was not permitted to sit down until she confessed. Then Miss Botting told the whole class that 'Jean' Frame – as she was called then – was a thief. The news spread around the school and around Wyndham, and at home Janet was strapped by her father. 'I was,' she wrote later, 'appalled by my future prospects . . .'

Those prospects improved dramatically, however, the following year. In February 1931 the Frames migrated north from Wyndham, population 700, to Oamaru, population 7000. Oamaru had been the family's first home town in New Zealand and birthplace of Janet's father. Here she accumulated memories of a very different kind that would lead her, many years later, to call the town her 'kingdom by the sea'.

The Frame siblings
restrained and
contained in Wyndham
for a family portrait
(from left): Myrtle,
Geordie, Janet,
Isabel and June.
ALEXANDER TURNBULL LIBRARY

Oamaru, the administrative centre of North Otago, had flourished in the late nineteen hundreds and declined in the early decades of the twentieth century. In the 1870s and 1880s it had become wealthy as a result of the export of wool, grain and meat. To reflect their wealth and optimism, the early town fathers had raised a succession of mercantile and public buildings in classical and Renaissance styles, most of them built or finished in the region's distinctive creamy-white limestone. The founders proudly spoke of Oamaru as the 'Athens of the South'. There was talk of it becoming, not merely the commercial capital of the South Island but also, ultimately, its political capital.

By the 1930s these dreams had died. Most of the region's meat, wool and dairy products were now exported from better-formed harbours to the north and the south (the port of Oamaru was no more than a natural headland with an artificial breakwater). Oamaru survived as a centre for servicing the farming district of North Otago, and it did have pockets of wealth. But the scale and character of the early buildings now seemed excessive. They were being progressively abandoned as the town's main street developed more modestly in a different direction, and grass grew between the cobblestones in the harbour precinct. This led

Janet, when she walked there, to regard it as a ghost city and to shiver with 'a sense of yesterdays'.

Because the worldwide depression of the late 1920s and early 1930s had knocked the bottom out of the British agricultural market, farmers had stopped spending money and the businesses who catered for them were forced to lay off staff and in some instances to close. In February 1931 Oamaru had a high rate of unemployment. As in Wyndham, vagrants would occasionally go from door to door in search of food and paid chores.

George Frame, now a fully-fledged engine driver, was never out of work through this period. But he did have his wages reduced by almost half on one occasion as a penalty for driving his engine through a red light. This caused his family considerable hardship and resulted in 'luxury items' (his 'Tin Lizzie' Ford car, his golf clubs, his bagpipes) being sold. Later, a reduction in working hours and overtime reduced his wage packet yet again.

The family found a modest house to rent at 56 Eden Street, in one of the town's 'blue collar' neighbourhoods. The roof was leaking, the weatherboards rotting, some of the sash

George Frame driving a steam engine, the job he was given as a permanent position when he and his family lived in Wyndham. The promotion came more than twenty years after he had joined the Railways as a cleaner.
JANET FRAME

The Frame grand-parents, Mary and Alex, as Janet knew them in her early childhood. Granddad Frame was living with the family when he died in 1931. Grandma Frame, who had become a double amputee because of circulation problems, had predeceased him.
JANET FRAME

window frames broken and panes cracked. There were cockroaches, slaters and earwigs in occupation. But the house also had four bedrooms, a sitting-room, a kitchen, a bathroom, a scullery; and a semi-detached washhouse and flush lavatory (the family's first). It was the most spacious house in which the family had ever lived, and it provided an affordable and secure arena for Frame family life and rites of passage for the next thirteen years.

The four Frame girls shared one bedroom and one double bed, top-and-tailing. Brother Geordie had a room to himself, as did Lottie and George, and Granddad Frame, who had come to live with them in the wake of his wife's death (he himself was to die at Eden St in September 1931). The real bonus for the Frame children, however, was the wider neighbourhood. The house backed on to a bull paddock and a creek. Behind these lay a

The Bank of Otago, which opened in 1871, exemplified the commercial optimism of Oamaru's town fathers in the last decades of the nineteenth century. A later commentator was to call it 'a strayed Greek temple' and noted that, typically for Oamaru, its depth was only half its frontal width.
North Otago Museum

The modest Frame home at 56 Eden Street, Oamaru, where the family lived for thirteen of Janet's childhood and adolescent years. One 'planny' is visible on the hill reserve behind.
JANET FRAME

grassed hill reserve with zigzag paths, a pine plantation ('the planny') and a seat on the summit, from which it was possible to see across the town's landmarks and out to sea.

Janet would write later that in Oamaru she became

> vividly aware of myself as a person
> on earth, feeling a kinship with other
> creatures and full of joy at the sights
> and sounds about me and drunk with
> the anticipation of play, where playing
> seemed endless, on and on after school
> until dark, when even then there were
> games to play in bed – physical games like

'trolly works' and 'fitting in', where each body curled into the other and all turned on command, or guessing games or imagining games . . . There were arguments and fights and plans for the future and impossible dreams of fame as dancers, violinists, pianists, artists.

The three oldest children were within easy walking distance of Oamaru North School and George Frame cycled to work each day to the railway yards and locomotive sheds. At school, Janet made her very first friend, Poppy Firman, who lent her a copy of *Grimms' Fairy Tales*. Janet read this book to her sisters in an ecstasy of discovery and excitement.

[Suddenly] the world of living and the world of reading became linked in a way I had not noticed before . . . [We] were the Dancing Princesses – not twelve but four; and as I read I saw in my mind . . . orchards hung with silver and golden apples, boughs that spoke and sang and cried out, underground seas and rivers and splash splash through the dark caverns, then suddenly the lit palace and the ballroom . . . None of [the characters] were more nor less than we were for all the lists of extraordinary gifts, miracles, transformations, cruelties, and the many long years of wandering and searching, full of hope and expectation.

There were few other books at 56 Eden St at this time – a *Bible* and a Christadelphian manual, from which Lottie Frame continued to read to her increasingly restless children on Sunday afternoons; a volume Janet remembered as 'the doctor's book', a 'lurid account of the human body in sickness'; and the collected works of Oscar Wilde, which George Frame had bought as part of an auction lot in Wyndham.

Janet's other reading came from comics (*My Favourite* and *Rainbow*); and the journals and

school readers available at Oamaru North School. It was in one of the latter that she discovered the word 'island', and went on thinking of it as 'is-land', a metaphor for present time, even when the phenomenon of the silent 's' had been explained to her. She also loved the poems, 'full of mystery and wonder', published in the *School Journals*: the works of John Keats, Walter de la Mare, John Drinkwater, Christina Rossetti, Alfred Noyes and John Masefield. Among the many she learned by heart was Keats' 'Meg Merrilees'. 'When I thought of Meg, I felt the sadness that came with the way the words went in the poem, the same way words went in songs about Glasgow and the sidewalks of New York and the streets of Dublin . . .'

Despite the excitements that came with reading, playing, discovering, exploring the hill behind their home, there were sadnesses too in the life of the Frame family: the deaths of Granddad Frame and later Auntie Maggie, who came to stay when she was dying of cancer of the throat; and the plight of brother Geordie who, at the age of nine, began to suffer from epileptic seizures. No drugs were available at this time to mitigate the condition. Instead Geordie was given large doses of bromide, which only increased his confusion and fear.

[Each] day at home there were episodes of violent rage when he attacked us or threw whatever was at hand to throw. There had usually been somewhere within the family to find a 'place', however cramped; now there seemed to be [none] . . . Mother, resisting fiercely the advice of the doctor to put [him] in an institution, nursed him while we girls tried to survive on our own.

In the process of surviving, the behaviour of the three younger Frame sisters – Myrtle had by this time left school and gone to work for Mrs McGimpsey, an Eden St widow with three children – sometimes seemed to outsiders to be out of control. 'We were not civilised,' Janet wrote later. '[We] giggled at Sunday Bible readings [which Lottie then abandoned], we wolfed our food, stuck out our elbows, did not come when called at bedtime, refused to fetch a shovel of coal when asked to: we ran wild and pulled faces and said Bum and Fart and Fuck.' Such behaviour led some Oamaru parents to forbid their offspring to play with the Frame girls. Janet lost her friendship with Poppy, and the mother of another would-be friend turned her away at the door.

All of which simply made the sisters more

Janet and Myrtle outside the washhouse at Eden Street, c. 1932: 'feral children who ran wild, did not come when called, pulled faces and said Bum and Fart and Fuck.' JANET FRAME

dependent on their own company, games and pastimes. And one of those pastimes, which had begun to flourish while Janet was still at primary school, was writing their own stories and poems. Soon, with their mother's encouragement, all five Frame children were writing for 'Dot's Little Folks' page in the *Otago Daily Times*, Janet under the name 'Amber Butterfly'.

Oh mushroom, white upon the ground,
How did you come to grow,
Making not one tiny sound
Within the earth below?
Were you at the fairies' ball

Clothed in snow-white sheen?
How did you come to grow at all
Upon the grasses green?

When, at the end of 1934, Janet was awarded the dux's medal at Oamaru North School, she also won a year's subscription to the town library, known as the 'Athenaeum'. This brought, for the first time, a flood of books into 56 Eden St, something for each member of the family: Charles Dickens, Mark Twain, Henry Longfellow, John Greenleaf Whittier for Lottie – who was still writing and publishing poetry of her own; 'something about the sea' for

31

Apparently tamed, the Frame girls pose in the Oamaru Public Gardens in new Christmas dresses from Aunty Polly.
JANET FRAME

her father; *Just William* books for Geordie. All this satisfied what Janet would later call 'print starvation'.

At Waitaki Junior High School, where she was enrolled in 1935, Janet was given further encouragement to write by a form teacher, Catherine Lindsay. Her mother's example and the gift from her father of Railways notebooks in which to record her own work, led her to decide in 1936 that she would become a poet when she 'grew up'. And her first place in English that year seemed an appropriate result for a future writer. She looked forward to following Myrtle to Waitaki Girls High School where the range of writers she would study, and the interest and complexity of their work, would increase significantly. Her parents did not think for a moment that their clever second daughter was destined to be a poet or, indeed, any other kind of writer. But they did want her to attend and – unlike Myrtle – to complete secondary school; because, like 'Cousin Peg in Canada', she was bright enough to be a teacher. And that was a prospect her parents thought was highly satisfactory.

The Oamaru North School's athletics team, 1934. Janet poses second on the right from her beloved teacher, Reuben Eutycus Dimick. In this her final primary school year, she won the dux medal and a year's free subscription to the town library. North Otago Museum

First, however, in the summer of 1936/37, the family took a camping holiday on the bank of the Rakaia River. There George pursued his favourite hobby, catching salmon with flies he had made himself. Lottie cooked, washed clothes, kept the billy boiling and wrote poems. The Frame children, joined by their friend from over the road at Eden St, Marguerite Miller, 'explored, played, ate'. There was a moment of anxiety for the highly superstitious Lottie when holiday photographs were developed and Myrtle appeared to be fading out of the back of a family group. They had already been told that she had a weak heart. But, as Myrtle always seemed so 'unmistakably present', it was unthinkable that she should not be there.

The opening of the 1937 school year was delayed by an outbreak of poliomyelitis. On 5 March, a day when Myrtle went swimming at the Oamaru Public Baths, Janet was poring over her new textbooks at the kitchen table. A stranger came to the door and announced that he was a doctor. 'I've come to tell you about your daughter Myrtle,' he said to Lottie. 'She's been drowned. They've taken her body to the morgue.' This news, entirely unexpected despite warnings about Myrtle's heart, was the great shock and the defining event of Janet's adolescent years. It meant

Janet at Eden Street with one of her father's salmon. JANET FRAME

George Frame with a bag of Waitaki salmon; and his home-made flies and flybook.
MAY WILLIAMSON/
REG GRAHAM

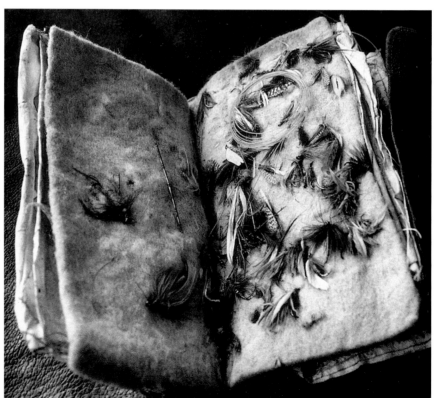

The Frames and Marguerite Miller camp on the bank of the Rakaia River in January 1937. Myrtle, allowed at last to wear slacks, appears ominously transparent at the back. JANET FRAME

the entire removal of Myrtle, not just for a holiday or next door or downtown or anywhere in the world, but off the face of the earth and out of the world . . . [My] teasing, pinching, thumping elder sister who knew more than I and would some day have made music, boys, clothes, love, a mansion . . . [Her] removal was stressed when she didn't come home that night to do the things she ordinarily did, to finish what she had begun in the morning, bring in the shoes cleaned with white cleaner and left to dry on the wash-house windowsill in the sun.

After Myrtle's funeral, Janet began to read the poetry book that would provide the basis for her early secondary school study of literature, *Mount Helicon*. To her amazement she discovered that many of the poets represented there seemed to know about her sister's death and about how strange life was without her. '[In] each day there was a blankness, a Myrtle-missing part, and it was upon this blankness that the poets in Mount Helicon were writing the story of my feelings.'

One of these was Edgar Allan Poe, whose poem 'Annabel Lee' seemed to express exactly what Janet was feeling:

For the moon never beams without
   bringing me dreams
Of the beautiful Annabel Lee;
And the stars never rise but I see the
   bright eyes
Of the beautiful Annabel Lee . . .

I was a child and she was a child,
In this kingdom by the sea:
But we loved with a love that was more
   than love —
I and my Annabel Lee . . .

The words 'kingdom by the sea' clinched for Janet the fact that the poet was addressing her directly, for that was how she thought of Oamaru with 'its wild sea beyond the break-water and the friendly bay safe within, with the sound of the sea in our ears day and night'. From this time on, 'kingdom by the sea' characterised for Janet her home town. It linked Oamaru inextricably to the loss of Myrtle, and it invested the town, and with it the whole temporal world, with the kinds of associations she would find in poetry. Myrtle's death confirmed her ambition to be a poet, and pointed her to the consolations she would find in the world of poetic imagination.

Janet was to remember her secondary school

Photograph of
Myrtle with (right)
a posthumously
constructed arm.
JANET FRAME

years at Waitaki Girls High School as, for the most part, unhappy ones. This was partly because she entered the school under the shadow of Myrtle's death, partly because of her continuing anxieties about items of her school uniform which, being home-made, never seemed quite to fit or to look 'normal'. These were also years in which she had no close friends, and in which she had difficulties coming to terms with the physical manifestations of menstruation and slowly rotting teeth.

Janet continued to write, however, in an effort to have 'my [own] place . . . undisturbed by outward pressures and expectations'. She kept a diary addressed to the bearded ruler of an imaginary land she called Ardenue. She became a contributor to 'Dot's Senior Page' in the *Otago Daily Times*, and she had poems published in the children's section of the *Oamaru Mail*, where she used the Maori-sounding nom de plume Amera, a near-anagram of Frame. She entered a competition sponsored by the radio station 3YA and had the satisfaction of hearing her winning poem broadcast. She had other verse published in *Truth*, the *Dairy Exporter* and *Railways Magazine*, and one of these subsequently appeared in an anthology of writing by New Zealand children.

Janet in the 'disastrous' junior high school uniform cobbled together by an unskilled Lottie Frame, 1935.
JANET FRAME

RIGHT: **It was at Waitaki Girls Junior High School that Janet began to give serious attention to the writing of poems and stories, largely for 'Dot's Little Folk', the children's page in the *Otago Daily Times*. And she began to collect annual prizes bestowed by the redoubtable Miss Jessie Banks Wilson, 'Lady Principal'.**
REG GRAHAM

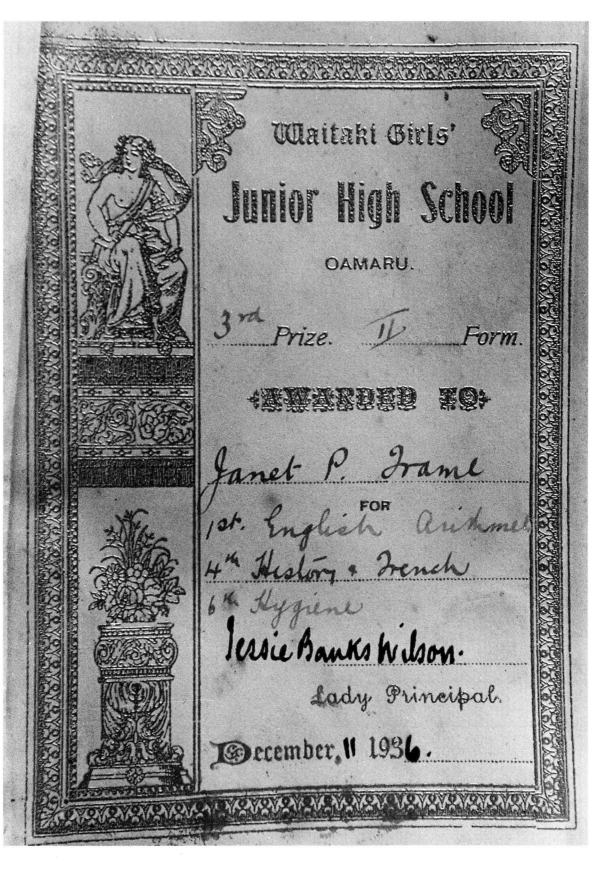

Waitaki Girls'

Junior High School

OAMARU.

3rd Prize. II Form.

AWARDED TO:

Janet P. Frame

FOR

1st. English Arithmetic

4th History & French

6th Hygiene

Jessie Banks Wilson.

Lady Principal.

December, 11 1936.

At home, Isabel and June were also writing poems. And all three sisters attempted to write novels in exercise books ('There Is Sweet Music', 'Go Shepherd', 'The Vision of the Dust'). In one of Janet's 1937 school prize books, *Boys and Girls Who Became Famous*, the sisters discovered the story of the Brontës and made it their own.

> We felt close to the self-contained family with the 'wild' brother, the far-off parents going about their daily tasks, the Brontës with their moors, us with our hill and gully and pine plantations. They knew death in their family, as we had, and their lives were so much more tragic than [ours] that we could give them, thankfully, the sad feelings which some-times overcame us . . . I felt that life was very serious now. I thought sometimes, with curiosity and apprehension, about the state known as the future.

That future, for Janet, was being inexorably mapped out by her teachers and by her parents. Her examination results were good, and she consistently topped her class in English and French and, in 1940, she was *proxime accessit* or runner-up to the dux of the school, her old rival Wendy Patterson. In 1942, her last year at Waitaki Girls High School, she was a prefect and captain of Gibson House. All this, her mentors agreed, pointed towards tertiary education and the projected career in teaching. That 1942 class had dwindled to four scholars, all of whom were now preparing themselves for university, teachers' college or both. 'We were like young birds on the edge of a cliff; wings fluttering; the air . . . filled with rustlings and testings and chatterings.'

And yet, ominously, Janet slid into a pit of depression in that final school year. She was still subject to waves of unresolved grief about Myrtle's death. She was anxious about the effects of the Second World War, which had already taken the lives of family friends and neighbours and which, with the entry of Japan, seemed to threaten the security of New Zealand itself. There were severe tensions at home where her epileptic brother Geordie, who had discovered alcohol, seemed locked in con-tinuous argument with their father. Her front teeth were now visibly decaying and the family could not afford visits to the dentist. And her ill-fitting school uniform was not only patched but also pressed uncomfortably on every part of her body.

As the year advanced, Janet seemed to be

heading for some kind of breakdown. 'I am convinced that I shall commit suicide soon,' she wrote in her diary. 'There is no bodily pain . . . I [just] want to cry and cry at the slightest sadness.' And later: 'I will die. I will commit suicide. Why should I live? I hate myself.' Her exam results at the end of that year were the weakest of her entire school career.

What interrupted the cycle of depression was a dramatic change in circumstance and location. Her application for Dunedin Teachers' Training College was accepted. And in February 1943 Janet returned to Dunedin, the city in which she had been born, to undergo teacher training and attend university lectures part-time. As an act of ritual separation from her 'old' life, she burned her notebooks of poems and all but one of her Ardenue diaries.

Janet (back right) in Waitaki Girls High School uniform. Her main rival for academic honours, Wendy Patterson, is at front left.
WENDY PATTERSON

CHAPTER TWO SEASON OF PERIL

I inhabited a territory of loneliness which . . . resembles that place where the dying spend their time before death and from where those who do return living to the world bring inevitably a unique point of view that is a nightmare, a treasure, and a lifelong possession . . . [It] must be the best view in the world, ranging even further than the view from the mountains of love, equal in its rapture and chilling exposure, there in the neighbourhood of the ancient gods and goddesses.

(JANET FRAME: AN ANGEL AT MY TABLE)

The University of
Otago, modelled on
Glasgow University, is
one of many buildings
in Dunedin that reflect
the city's Scottish
character and origins.
Janet became a part-
time student here,
of English and French,
while undertaking her
teacher training.
HOCKEN LIBRARY

Janet (middle, back
row) as part of the
Dunedin Teachers'
College student body.
GREGOR MACAULAY

JANET FRAME HAD BEEN STEERED TOWARDS teaching because her academic record seemed commensurate with a career of that kind and because, apart from librarianship and nursing, there were few other career openings for clever young women at this time. Her acceptance for a place at Dunedin Teachers' Training College may have been influenced by the fact that her cousin Iona Livingston had already been an outstandingly good student there. Janet, however, was no Iona. Her shyness, her lack of social confidence and her low level of social skills, all these qualities made her a risky candidate for the teaching profession, a fact which her supervisors eventually recognised.

Her first year of training, however, went moderately well. She enjoyed the college teaching programme – English, history, geography, music, arts, crafts, physical education – and she alternated it with lectures at university in English and French. Within weeks of starting, her whole life was filled up with the need to attend classes and lectures, and to study and read. She struck up a friendship with two contemporaries from Waitaki Girls High School, Katherine Bradley and Rona Pinder, and with an equally shy girl from Stewart Island, Sheila Traill.

The highlight of each week was her university English lectures from Professor Herbert

Ramsay and Gregor Cameron. Janet became wholly engaged by their resonant analyses of Shakespeare, Chaucer, *Beowulf* and *Piers Plowman*. Every line of *Measure for Measure* '[stirred] in me a host of ideas, crowding avenues of dreaming, lines of poems . . .'

Boarding arrangements were less satisfactory. Janet was paying ten shillings a week to live with her father's sister, Aunty Isy Renwick, and her husband George. Her room in their tiny brick cottage was small and looked out on brick walls and chimneys. The whole house was cold, and the meals provided by Aunty Isy as part of the board were frugal. Janet, trying to live up to Aunty Isy's view of her as a 'nice girl, no trouble at all', made no complaint. To make home life even more gloomy, Uncle George was confined to bed, dying (as it turned out) from lung cancer.

One symptom of her excessive shyness was the fact that Janet was too embarrassed to burn her soiled sanitary towels at the Renwicks'. Instead she stuffed them into drawers until the smell became too unpleasantly obvious. Then she took them to the Southern Cemetery, which ran along the ridge at the top of Carroll St, and stuffed them into cracks and crevices. The cemetery also became 'her place' to be alone, to

dream, to think about her studies, and to compose experimental poems influenced by her reading of Gerard Manley Hopkins, Dylan Thomas and George Barker.

Giotto alone through
serious red roofs
and social gravity of smoke
sees St Francis
by the watered rock

but here the passage of city bells
is explored
by no Giotto
to the final resting water

only limping he passes
from the woman crying
'noli me tangere'
to St Francis alone in the Octagon,
under the sycamore trees
given alas no pathetic honouring

Back home in Eden St, Oamaru, the gap between Janet and her family was widening. The unpleasantness between her father and brother had intensified. Her mother took refuge in her religion, and in unrealistic and irrelevant dreams (such as wanting each of her surviving daughters to have a white fox fur on their twenty-first birthdays). Her two younger

46

As Janet focused on
her first year of teacher
training and university
study in 1943, her sister
Isabel (left) was turning
out to be 'fearless,
adventurous, rebellious,
a rule-breaker', just as
Myrtle had been.
JANET FRAME

sisters were preoccupied with school and with their own friends, and Janet felt excluded from their lives. And she was infuriated by what she believed to be her parents' 'ignorance':

> They knew nothing of Sigmund Freud, of *The Golden Bough*, of T. S. Eliot . . . Overwhelmed with the flood of new knowledge I was bursting with information about the Mind, the Soul, the Child . . . All were described, measured, labelled, expounded in detail to my bewildered parents . . . I could now say to members of my family, 'That's rationalisation, that's sublimation, you're really frustrated sexually, your superego tells you but your id disagrees.' Mother blushed when I said the word 'sexually'. Dad frowned and said nothing except, 'So that's what you learn at University and Training College . . .'

Home life took on a whole new character for Janet when, at the beginning of her second year of teacher training, the family moved out of Eden St (which was sold from under them) and into Willowglen, a property on the outskirts of town. This, unexpectedly, George Frame was able to buy, thanks to winning a building society ballot of three hundred dollars,

TOP: **Early in 1944 the Frames were forced to shift from Eden Street to Willowglen, a run-down property on the outskirts of Oamaru. The family was now literally as well as metaphorically on the margins of the town.** NORTH OTAGO MUSEUM

RIGHT: **While Willowglen looked attractive at certain times of the year, especially when the fruit trees were in blossom, Janet never 'bonded' with the property or regarded it as home. And the house was too small to contain family tensions.** JANET FRAME

which he used as a deposit. Janet, however, was not pleased. She liked neither the size nor the character of the 'new' house:

I felt depressed and lonely and I knew [Willowglen] would never be my home; it was too small, everyone was too close to everyone else; in the front bedroom you could hear the wireless from the kitchen as if you were in the kitchen. You could hear the arguments too, the raised voices, and the soft murmur of pleading that you knew to be, 'Don't raise your voices to each other,' from Mother.

That year, 1944, had begun badly. It was to get worse. Isabel accompanied Janet back to Dunedin, where she too would train as a teacher. While Janet had been prepared to endure living conditions at Aunty Isy's (George Renwick had died in the course of the previous year), her younger sister was not. When eventually, Aunty Isy discovered that her nieces had been supplementing their meagre diets by eating the chocolates she had won in Highland dancing competitions, recriminations flew. Isabel left for private board, and Janet moved into Stuart House, a university hostel.

The day the cow looked in the front door at Willowglen.
JANET FRAME

Partly to compensate for this upheaval, she threw herself into her college work with renewed determination. She wrote a children's story, 'Keel and Kool'*, for her literature class. The lecturer, Joan Stevens, summoned Janet for congratulations and asked if she had considered becoming a writer for children. A major assignment she wrote for her social studies class was not as well received. She prepared it as 'a geographical and social version of [Virginia Woolf's novel] *The Waves*, with bizarre illustrations cut from magazines . . .' Staff opinion was divided between those like librarian Dorothy Neal White, who thought it brilliant; and those like the lecturer in charge, Arthur 'Agony' Payne, who did not. Mr Payne's assessment prevailed.

Janet summoned the courage to submit two poems to the college magazine, *Te Rama*. This time opinions were divided between those who thought them brilliant and others who considered them spoofs. The advocates of genius prevailed, and Janet won a ten-shilling prize for one of them, 'Cat':

Deaf to the hammering window
and the idiot boy's mewing,

I leave the torn mice to flow
in his vacant eyes
and sit propped up by a fat thinking;

but the will of the beating boy
burgles my ear, creeps
like a curled cat in my brain,
purrs and sleeps
and pads me from the house
to the scratched clouds and the clawed
   moon . . .

and the winds like torn mice
flow through my vacant eyes

At university she continued her study of English, this time more Shakespeare and an elementary look at Old English. She scored 75 percent in one term's examination and 40 in the other. In contrast to her A grade for the previous year, in 1944 she received a simple pass.

Janet also passed the training college examinations with an overall grading of 63 percent. Her final assessment, based on exams and periods 'on section' teaching in local schools, noted that she was, 'An unusual type; brilliant scholar in languages and a highly intelligent

* This is not the story of Frame's of the same name published later in *The Lagoon and Other Stories*.

person . . . but temperamentally something of a risk.' But nobody suggested to her that, on the basis of that assessment, she should do anything other than teach. And so, after the summer vacation, Janet returned to Dunedin late in January 1945 to begin her year's probationary teaching at Arthur St School. If she obtained satisfactory reports from the headmaster and the inspector who would visit her class in the course of that year, she would become a certified teacher. Janet knew what was at stake, she wanted to succeed; but she was also terrified by the spectre of what lay ahead.

She boarded that year with Mrs Elizabeth Wadsworth, a widow who lived in the suburb of Maori Hill. Mrs Wadsworth's house was everything that Willowglen wasn't: it was carpeted, floral wallpapered, furnished with upholstered sofas and chairs that retained their stuffing, it was replete with ornaments and knick-knacks, and it was clean. The effect, Janet would write later, was one of 'comfort with an air of concealment'.

She continued her university studies by taking a paper in psychology, which was taught principally by John Money, a strikingly handsome young junior lecturer. Janet referred to him as 'Ash', after the fair-haired Ashley Wilkes

played by Leslie Howard in the film *Gone with the Wind*. Money's lectures and laboratory sessions, held on two evenings and on Saturday mornings, became highlights of her week. Soon too she was attending Money's weekly sessions

John Money, the handsome psychology lecturer on whom Janet developed a 'pash' in 1945. John Money

in musical appreciation, at which he played records and talked about the great composers and their music. Janet's enjoyment of psychology and music and, in particular, of the sight and sound of her favourite lecturer, were sufficiently strong to renew her stamina for the job she *wasn't* enjoying – indeed, a job that, as the year progressed, she began to dread and then to hate.

It wasn't the teaching or the company of children that Janet found troublesome. She was at ease in the presence of her class of thirty eight- and nine-year-olds and stimulated by daily contact with them. What she feared was interaction with other teachers, the unannounced visits to the classroom of the headmaster, Mr C. D. Gilling, and the prospect of a major inspection by an education board official before the end of the year.

Janet developed strategies to cope with these difficulties. She avoided staff members by avoiding the staffroom. Instead of having lunches and morning and afternoon teas with her colleagues, she took to staying in her classroom with the excuse that she was preparing work for the next teaching sessions. And, to satisfy the headmaster, she invented 'a serial story which I could continue whenever I heard the steps of authority approaching along the corridor, so that a visit by the headmaster to a class sitting rapt with attention . . . might "prove" my ability as a teacher'. About the looming visit of the inspector, however, she could do nothing except anticipate it and fear it.

In July 1945, everything that was preoccupying Janet and generating anxiety – her sense of isolation, the tension she experienced at school, her apprehension about the future, her 'pash' on John Money – all combined to produce a crisis. A new lecturer took over the Saturday morning psychology laboratory classes. This development, which appeared to eliminate her weekend contact with Money, and hence her major source of pleasure and replenishment, coincided with a particularly unhappy week at school. Janet decided to commit suicide.

Her landlady was away for the weekend. Janet tidied her room, swallowed a packet of aspirin with the help of several glasses of water, and lay down on her bed to die. She did not die, however. She woke up the following morning with a roaring noise in her ears, a severe nosebleed and a need to vomit. She recovered sufficiently to face her returned landlady that evening and to go to school the following day, as if nothing had happened.

The following month, August 1945, was especially eventful. The Second World War ended on 14 August with the surrender of Japan. Janet 'came of age' on the twenty-eighth by turning twenty-one. She also wrote her first adult short story, 'University Entrance', which she sent to the *New Zealand Listener* (it would be published seven months later, in March 1946). And she completed a biographical assignment for Money's class in which she mentioned, as if it were a casual afterthought, 'a recent attempt at suicide', and gave the clinical term for asprin, acetylsalicylic acid, to make the attempt sound more serious.

The reference to suicide in her assignment had the effect Janet probably intended: it worried John Money, who also had responsibility for dealing with students exhibiting emotional or 'psychological' difficulties. He called her to his office on 19 September, ostensibly to discuss her assignment as a whole but in fact to assess her state of mental health. What he heard from his clever but erratic student alarmed him.

Janet told Money that she had walked out of her classroom at Arthur St the previous week just as the inspector had walked in. This was in part a consequence of her deep fear of being judged, she said. But it was related to the fact that, the previous day, Money had passed her in the street without recognising her. She had trouble teaching, she said, because of 'bright ideas' flitting through her mind (were these, Money wondered, hallucinations?). And she had a 'deep devotion' to literature, which was far stronger than her ability or her wish to teach. In fact, she wanted to extricate herself from teaching for good. She had also told her headmaster that she would produce a medical certificate to explain her sudden departure from the classroom and her continuing absence from the school. But of course she had no such certificate, and that had become an additional source of anxiety.

To Janet's relief, Money took all this seriously and, indeed, took control of her predicament. He spoke with both her headmaster and the Education Board inspector. They agreed that Frame should return to school without any penalty, see out the teaching year, and then be judged unsuited for teaching, which would leave her free to seek other employment. Meanwhile she would have weekly counselling sessions with the psychology lecturer or see him more frequently if she so wished.

Frame's pleasure at this outcome was focused largely on the fact that she had engaged the attention of the man with whom she had become obsessed, and that she would now be able to meet with him frequently on a one-to-one basis. She was even prepared, she said later, to manufacture symptoms of a psychological nature to retain his interest. What she was not happy about was the proviso that she should remain at Arthur St School until the end of the year.

Two weeks later, when Money had left a message rescheduling a meeting with her until after the weekend, Janet rang him from a public telephone to say that she had walked out of school again and proposed to commit suicide. Money arranged for the police to collect her and bring her to his office, and for George Frame and Isabel to be with her over the coming weekend. Her explanation for her behaviour was that she had felt desperate when Money had postponed their appointment.

A week later there was a further incident of this kind. Money consulted with his colleagues, and they agreed that Janet needed supervision and rest to see her through an emotionally tumultuous period. They felt certain she would stabilise once she no longer had to attend Arthur St School. And so that evening, 18 October 1945, they persuaded her to enter the psychiatric ward at Dunedin Hospital. Janet's reaction to this measure was benign:

> I suddenly felt free of all worry, cared for. I could think of nothing more desirable than lying in bed sheltered and warm, away from teaching and trying to earn money, and even away from Mrs [Wadsworth] and her comfortable home; and away from my family and my worry over them; and from my increasing sense of isolation in a brave bright world of brave bright people; away from . . . being twenty-one and responsible . . .

Janet's life had now been deflected from the orbit that had propelled her towards teaching, regardless of whether or not she had wanted to teach. Now, by agreeing to enter hospital, she was to be propelled with even greater force towards another destination that would prove even more destructive, and far more difficult to interrupt.

When, on 30 October, Lottie Frame arrived at Dunedin Hospital to take her to Willowglen, Janet panicked and began to scream at her mother:

> Faced suddenly with the prospect of going

home, I felt all the worries of the world returning, all the sadness of home and the everlasting toil of my parents and the weekly payments . . . and the arguments . . . I knew that home was the last place I wanted to be. I screamed at Mother to go away. She left, murmuring her bewilderment, 'But she's such a happy person, she's always been such a happy person.'

Janet had imagined that the alternative to going home would be to stay in Dunedin, to find a new job (perhaps as a librarian), and to continue with her writing. She was wrong. In the view of her hospital doctors, she was showing symptoms of what they, without telling her, had diagnosed as chronic schizophrenia. The alternative to public hospital care was incarceration in a mental hospital. And on 2 November 1945, Janet Frame was committed to Seacliff Hospital, a Victorian lunatic asylum with all the characteristics that designation implied.

Seacliff, as its name indicated, stood on a clifftop high above the coast about 30 kilometres north of Dunedin. Its tower and mock battlements were suggestive of a Gothic castle. It was constructed largely of stone and cement and

Seacliff Hospital high on the Otago coastline: a place of almost Gothic horror. ALEXANDER TURNBULL LIBRARY

was unheated. The slope on which it stood was subsiding gradually towards the sea, and almost every week sewer and water pipes broke and further cracks appeared in the walls and ceilings. The tools of psychiatric analysis were few and blunt at this time, and treatment at the hospital was confined largely to work therapy (sewing, cleaning, gardening), or to electro-convulsive or insulin shock therapy. For many of the 1200 patients incarcerated there, the institution was little better than an inadequately staffed prison. A fire that swept through one of the women's wards three years prior to Janet Frame's arrival had incinerated thirty-seven patients.

To allow a period of observation, Janet was assigned to a women's ward and given domestic duties in the nurses' home. None of the overworked nursing or medical staff spoke to her about her feelings or the causes of her 'breakdown', but they noted their impressions of her behaviour, viewed through the prism of schizophrenia which doctors at Dunedin Hospital had provided. 'This girl is most foolish and fatuous in her manner and conversation, grins foolishly when addressed and tends to inattention . . . [She is] quite unconcerned at being here and generally emotionally apathetic.'

This last comment was far from true. Janet's concern was considerable and she was profoundly shocked by much of what she saw as she wandered between her ward and the nurses' home:

> [I] peeped through the fence of a building called Simla . . . where there were strange men in striped shirts and trousers and some without trousers, walking round and round in a paddock with the grass worn away . . . [There] was a cart, like a rickshaw, that passed every day by the ward . . . full of coal and two men harnessed to the cart carried the coal, driven by one of the attendants . . . [I] peered into a room that stank of urine and was full of children lying in cots, strange children, some of them babies making strange noises; their faces wet with tears and snot . . . I saw people with their eyes staring like the eyes of hurricanes surrounded by whirling unseen and unheard commotion . . .

Seacliff, for Janet, was a place of horror, softened for her only by the compassion that she felt for so many of the inmates who were infinitely more damaged than she was. What was she doing there?

She was there because a variety of factors in her life had collided and produced a crisis. She had grown up in Oamaru believing that her family were outcasts and that she was 'different'; she had lost her beloved older sister when she was twelve and never grieved properly for that loss; she was awkward, unconfident and lacking in social skills; and she had taken refuge in literature to compensate for timidity and loneliness. Her relative lack of socialisation made her less mature than most of her contemporaries and as a consequence she had focused a kind of patho-logical love on her handsome and charming psychology lecturer. When there seemed no prospect that her feelings would be reciprocated, she had been gripped by a form of hysteria that generated apparently psychotic symptoms. And it was the effects of this hysteria that hospital psychiatrists had identified as schizophrenia.

In the course of this, the first six weeks that Janet spent in a mental hospital, there was to be no deterioration, no further crisis to confirm the diagnosis made in Dunedin Hospital. Instead, she was released into the care of her family just before Christmas 1945. After she and June had spent a holiday in the Marlborough Sounds with her mother's relations, Janet was even prepared to believe that nothing significant had happened to change her life. Then she came back to Oamaru, to confront some unpleasant surprises.

The first was that she had not been given a promised aegrotat pass for her previous year's work in psychology, so she still had only three units of the nine needed for a degree. The second was being told by her bank that she was not to have access to her own money – 'I was officially insane and would not have legal rights until my "probation" . . . ended, and then only if

Home again in Oamaru after her first sojourn in Seacliff. Weeks later Janet would be in Dunedin making her first serious attempt to live as a writer. JANET FRAME

the doctor declared my sanity.' And the final blow was being told at Oamaru Hospital, for the first time, that she was schizophrenic. The doctor who conveyed this gave no explanation of the illness, so she had to look it up herself in one of her psychology textbooks. There it was described as a gradual deterioration of mind and behaviour with no cure. And this she had discovered just at the point where she had begun to feel that she had recovered from whatever crisis had sent her to hospital. 'It seemed to spell my doom.'

For a time, doom was kept at bay by the need to make practical arrangements. Janet did not wish to live at Willowglen, where the tension between her father and her brother was still palpable. What she wanted was an occupation that would enable her to pay her way in the world, but leave time for study, reading and writing. She advertised for a 'live-in' job in Dunedin and found one with Mrs T. Park of Caversham, who ran a combined boarding house and rest-home. Janet would be paid fifteen shillings a week plus her 'keep' to look after four elderly women who, each morning, had to be washed, toileted and fed. Her afternoons and evenings would be free for her own work which, she told Mrs Park, was 'private research'.

Her room at 63 Playfair St was a converted linen cupboard with a bed, some shelves and a single small window with a dreary view. Here, from February 1946, Frame began to live independently for the first time in her life and, balanced on the narrow bed, to write stories partly influenced by the Californian writer William Saroyan ('I can do that too,' she had told herself when she read his stories). She was also influenced, for the first time, by New Zealand writers. At Modern Books, a left-wing

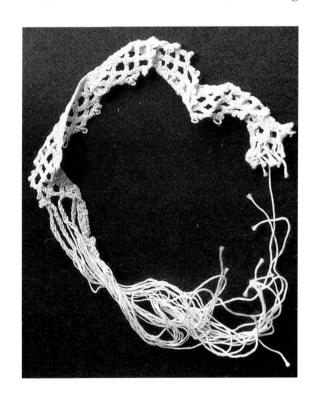

59

French lace made by Janet in hospital as an exercise in occupational therapy. Reg Graham

Dunedin bookshop, she bought three volumes that would have a pervasive influence on her future professional life: *A Book of New Zealand Verse 1923–45* edited by the Christchurch poet and journalist Allen Curnow; *Speaking for Ourselves*, an anthology of short stories collected by the Auckland fiction writer Frank Sargeson; and *Beyond the Palisade*, a collection of poems by the precocious and brilliant Dunedin writer James K. Baxter.

All three writers, Sargeson, Baxter and Curnow, were to have roles in her future life and work; as were some of the others in the anthologies, such as poets Charles Brasch and Denis Glover. At the time, though, these books served primarily to turn her attention away from the writers and landscapes of the Northern Hemisphere, and towards those in her own country. 'It was almost a feeling of having been an orphan who discovers that her parents are alive and living in the most desirable home . . .'

Her impulse to write was given momentum in March 1946 when her first short story for adults, 'University Entrance', appeared in the national journal the *New Zealand Listener*. It had grown out of the anxiety she had felt in her schooldays whenever she had had to ask her

parents for money. There were recognisably autobiographical elements: the portraits of her mother and father; the 'pash' on a teacher, Miss Macaulay (called Miss Heafy in the story); the depression she felt when she had to leave the world of literature at school and come home to face prosaic realities; and the constant anxiety about money.

Somewhat to her own surprise, Janet's reaction to the appearance of the story was ambivalent. On the one hand she was pleased to have been accepted for publication by the most prestigious journal in the country; on the other, she experienced what seemed like a phobia associated with seeing her own words in print (even though her own name was not used: she had asked to be identified simply as 'J. F.'). The experience was analogous to looking into a mirror and, Caliban-like, being frightened of what she might see there. Janet wanted to write; and she wanted to write well; and she wanted to be accepted as a writer. But she wasn't at all sure that she wanted to appear in print or be recognised as the author of particular stories. This paradox, rarely encountered in the community of writers, would create problems for her as her career unfolded.

The new stories she was writing at Caversham

Manuscript pages of 'The Lagoon', written for John Money in 1946. It became the title story for her first book. AUCKLAND UNIVERSITY LIBRARY

The Lagoon.

At low tide the water is sucked back into the harbour
and there is no lagoon, only a stretch of dirty grey sand
shaded with dark pools of sea-water where you may find
a baby octopus if you are lucky, or the spotted orange old
house of a crab or the drowned wreckage of a child's toy boat.
There is a bridge over the lagoon where you may look down into
the little pools and see your image tangled up with sea-water and
rushes and bits of cloud. And sometimes at night there is an under
water moon, dim and secret.

All this my grandmother told me, my Picton grandmother
who could cut suple jack and find kidney fern and make a track
through the thickest part of the bush. When my grandmother died
all the Maoris at the Pah came to her funeral, for she was a
friend of the Maoris, and her mother had been a Maori princess,
very beautiful they said, with fierce ways of loving and hating.

See the lagoon, my grandmother would say. xxxxxxxxxxxxx
The dirty lagoon, full of drifting wood and sea-weed and crabs' xxx
claws. It is dirty and sandy and smelly in summer. I remember we
used to skim round white stones over the water, and catch tiddlers
in the little creek near by, and make sand castles on the edge,
this is my castle we said, you be father I'll be mother and we'll
live here and catch crabs and tiddlers for ever.

I liked my grandmother to talk about the lagoon. And when I
went for a holiday to Picton where grandma lived I used to say
grandma tell me a story. About the Maori Pah. About the old man
who lived down the Sounds and had a goat and a cow for friends.
About the lagoon. And my grandmother would tell me stories of the
Sounds and the Pah and herself when she was young, being a girl
and going out to work in the rich people's houses. But the lagoon
never had a proper story, or if it had a proper story my
grandmother never told me.

See the water she would say. Full of sea-weed and crabs'
claws. But I knew that wasn't the real story and I didn't find
out the real story till I was grown-up and grandma had died
and most of the old Maoris were gone from the Pah, and the old man
and the cow and the goat were forgotten.

I went for a holiday to Picton. It was a long journey by
train and I was glad at the end of it to see the green and blue
town that I remembered from childhood, though it was smaller of
course and the trees had shrunk and the hills were tiny.

I stayed with an aunt and uncle. I went for launch rides
round the harbour and I went for picnics with summery people
in floral frocks and sun hats, and kids in print frocks, or
khaki shorts if they were boys, especially if they were boys
with fathers in the army. We took baskets with fruit and sand-
wiches, not tomato for tomato goes damp though some like it damp,
and threepences in the pocket for ice-creams. There were races for

the kiddies and some for the men and women, and afterwards a man
walked round the grounds throwing lollies in the air. They were
great days out picnicking in the Sounds with the Maoris singing
and playing their ukeleles, but they didn't sing the real Maori
songs, they sang you are my sunshine and South of the Border. And
then it got dark and the couples came back from the trees and
the launches were got ready and everybody went back singing, with
the babies crying because they were tired and sunburnt and bitten
by sandflies. Sandflies are the devil everybody said, but they
were great days they were great days for the kiddies.

Perhaps I kix liked the new Picton, I don't know. If there
were things I hadn't noticed before there were also things gone
that I thought would be there for ever. The Two gum trees that I
called the two ladies were gone or if they were there I couldn't
find them, and the track over the Domain Hill wasn't there. We
used to climb up and watch the steamer coming in from the straits.
And there was gorse mixed up with the bush, and the
bush itself didn't hold the same fear, even with its secret
terrible drippings and rustlings that go on for ever.

There were more people in the town too. The Main Trunk
Line brings more tourists, my aunt said. There were people every
-where, lying on the beach being burned or browned by the sun and
sea, people whizzing round the harbour, like the ᶦⁿ
pop-pop boats we used to whizz round in the bath on Christmas   *motor-boats*
morning. People surf-riding, playing tennis, fishing in the Strait
Straits, practising in skiffs for the Regatta. People.

But my grandmother wasn't there to
show me everything and tell me stories. And the Lagoon was dirtier
than ever. See the lagoon said my aunt. Full of drifting wood
and sea-weed and crabs' claws. We could see the lagoon from
the kitchen window. We were looking at photographs that day,
what silly clothes people wore in those days. There was grandma
sitting on the verandah with her knitting, and there was my
great grandmother, the Maori princess with her big brown eyes,
and her lace dress on that her husband bought her, handmade lace
said my aunt, he loved her till he met that woman from
Nelson, men are crazy sometimes, but I suppose
women are crazier.
- Is there a story, I said. I was a child again, grandma tell me
about..

My aunt smiled. She guesses things sometimes.
- The sort of story they put in Truth, she said. On the
morning of the tragedy witness saw defendent etc. etc. Your
great grandmother was a murderess. She drowned her husband, pushed
him in the lagoon. I suppose the tide was high, I don't know.
They would call it The Woman From Nelson,.. she mused. They
would have photos. But then nobody knew, only the family. Every
body thought he had had one over the eight and didn't know where
he was going.
My aunt drew aside the curtain and peered out. She reminded me of

the women in films who turn to the window in an emotional
moment, but the moment wasn't emotional nor was my aunt.
- It's an interesting story, she said. I prefer Dostoievsky to
Truth.
The water was brown and shining and to the right lay the dark
shadow of the Domain Hill. There were kids playing on the edge,
Chrisopher Robins with sand between the toes, sailing toy
warships and paddling with bare feet in the pools.
- Grandma never told me, I said.
Again my aunt smiled. The reason (she quoted) one talks farthest
from the heart is the fear that it may be hurt.
And then my aunt dropped the curtain xxxxxxxxx across the
window and turned to the photographs again.
Was it my aunt speaking or was it my grandmother or my great
grandmother who loved a white lace dress?
At low tide there is no lagoon. Only a strtch of dirty grey sand.
I remember we used to skim thin white stones over the water and ax
catch tiddlers in the little creek near by and make sand castles,
this is my castle we said you be father I'll be mother and we'll
live here and catch crabs and tiddlers for ever..

———————

drew largely on her childhood and family recollections. A smaller number grew out of her recent adult experience, at Seacliff and in the boarding house. She typed on a second-hand Barlock typewriter which she balanced on her knees while sitting on her bed. There was no room in the converted linen cupboard to work any other way. Her life away from Playfair St was given over to philosophy lectures in the evenings (her new university subject) and reading in the Dunedin Public Library.

By May 1946 she had resumed her weekly counselling sessions with John Money (legitimised by the fact that she was still a university student). And, as part of this routine, she began, from June 1946, to bring him one at a time the new stories she was writing. While Money was not especially 'literary', he recognised that they were good. He encouraged this activity and retained the manuscripts himself to ensure that they were not destroyed or lost by the author who, once they were finished, seemed to have little interest in their fate (it was the *act* of writing that was important to her, Janet would say later, not the business of publication). Janet also gave Money poems which he, seduced by that first professional diagnosis, described as 'pure schizophrenia'. He offered to find a publisher for the stories and

poems, and Janet, if she didn't actually actually encourage him to do so, did not discourage him either.

The first piece of work Money placed for her was a story called, initially, 'Alison Hendry'. It was one of the 'boarding house' sequence and included details from her real life, including a description of her room at Playfair St and glimpses of her time at Arthur St School, Dunedin Hospital and Seacliff. Money offered it to Charles Brasch, a Dunedin poet with private means who had returned to his home town of Dunedin from England in 1945 and announced that he planned to establish a serious literary quarterly journal. 'Alison Hendry' appeared in the second issue of *Landfall* (June 1947). It also appeared in Frame's first book, *The Lagoon and Other Stories*, in 1952. But by that time its original by-line, 'Jan Godfrey' (the first part of her own name combined with her mother's maiden name), had became the story's title.

Money also attempted to introduce Janet to Brasch, and to the brilliant and charismatic poet Baxter, seeking to create a circle of writerly friends for her. But in both instances she found herself unable to talk when she encountered them in Money's office ('I am a moron when people talk to me,' she said afterwards. 'My mind freezes.').

Money's primary ambition in relation to Janet's writing was to have her stories published as a collection. After seeking advice from a family friend, Anton Vogt, he gave the accumulated manuscript of twenty-four stories to the poet Denis Glover, who at that time owned and operated Caxton Press in Christchurch, which had published the three earlier volumes Janet had so much admired. By February 1947 Glover had undertaken to proceed with publication: 'I have not seen anything quite so unaffectedly natural and at the same time incisive for a long time,' he wrote. He was less keen to publish the poems, which he called 'brilliantly impressionistic, but very naive . . .'

This news pleased Janet, for it validated the

Reprieve: Janet (second from left) hams it up with the Bradley sisters and another friend on holiday on Stewart Island, January 1947. JANET FRAME

worth of the stories. But she was cautious. They were, she told Money, 'yours to arrange in any way you like, except that my name must never be mentioned.' She had had a busy summer, which included a holiday to Stewart Island with her old school and training college friends the Bradley sisters and Rona Pinder. And soon, she told Money, she was going to look after her father while her sister Isabel took Lottie Frame on a holiday back to Picton, their mother's old home town. She was mindful too that the tenth anniversary of Myrtle's death loomed in March 1947 and, as a consequence, 'the idea of death is with me all the time.'

The idea of death intruded far more forcefully than anyone could have predicted, however. On 17 February, in an unbelievable repetition of family tragedy, Isabel Frame drowned in Picton Harbour on what was the first full day of her holiday there. She too, it transpired, had had a heart defect. 'I almost cannot bear to be thinking that tonight outside in the dark I have two drowned sisters, even colder than live people,' Janet wrote to Money. And, a few days later:

> I think we are such sad small people,
> standing, each alone in a circle, trying
> to forget that death and terror are near.
> But death comes, and terror comes, and

then we join hands and the circle is really magic. We have the strength then to face terror and death, even to laugh and make fun of being alive, and after that even to make more music and writing and dancing. But always, deep down, we are small sad people standing humanly alone. Oh for the hands to be joined together for ever and the magic circle never to be broken . . .

The combined shocks of Isabel's death and the departure of John Money six months later, to what would become a highly successful career in the United States, resulted in a sharp deterioration in Janet's carefully nurtured sense of wellbeing. She moved from Dunedin to Christchurch, to be near a counsellor Money had recommended, Grete Christeller, a Jungian psychotherapist; and she became increasingly concerned about the state of her upper teeth, which by this time were well advanced in decay. Mrs Christeller booked her in to Christchurch Hospital to have the teeth removed. And, in a more complex decision, told Janet that her emotional and 'mental' problems might be helped by electro-convulsive therapy. 'She thinks my mind is so much divided that only a physical shock will unite it,' Janet reported to Money.

Another ominous family picture: Isabel (top left) fades out of a doubly-exposed photograph of her pupils at Windsor Primary School, 1947. JANET FRAME

Isabel in Picton, the day before she died: loud, assertive and unmistakably present. JANET FRAME

Lottie Frame at Willowglen, hat covering the hair that turned white the week Isabel died. JANET FRAME

Thus it was that in February 1948 Janet entered Sunnyside Hospital in Christchurch as a voluntary patient. Her letters to Money suggest that, at this time, her state of mind was close to that of the fictional narrator in her later novel, *Faces in the Water*, who spoke of entering a 'season of peril':

> [A] great gap opened in the ice floe between myself and other people whom I watched, with their world, drifting away through a violet-coloured sea where hammer-head sharks in tropical ease swam side by side with the seals and the polar bears. I was alone on the ice. A blizzard came and I grew numb and wanted to lie down and sleep and I would have done so had not the strangers arrived with scissors and cloth bags filled with lice and red-labelled bottles of poison . . . And the strangers, without speaking, put up circular calico tents and camped with me, surrounding me with their merchandise of peril.

For the next seven years Janet was in and out of mental hospitals – Sunnyside, Seacliff, Avondale, but principally Seacliff – with the regularity of a swinging pendulum. She would have shock treatment, which terrified her,

Lottie, from the Willowglen washhouse, attempts to coax her beloved fantails. JANET FRAME

recover from it, be sent home to Willowglen on probation; and then, after weeks or months, the tensions at home would drive her back into hospital, sometimes voluntarily.

These years were far from featureless, though – because of the ECT – she sometimes had difficulty in retrospect distinguishing one hospital committal from another. There were peaks and troughs. One of the troughs was a terrible night in Park House, Avondale Hospital, where she lay among human beings who had been transformed into living as animals. On that occasion, sleepless among the howls of the demented and the stench of urine, she came as close as she ever would to losing belief in her own identity and hope that she had any kind of future. She rolled on her straw mattress to face the darkened wall and recited the Twenty-third Psalm:

> The Lord is my shepherd: I shall
>   not want.
> He maketh me to lie down in green
>   pastures:
> He leadeth me beside the still waters.
> Yea, though I walk through the valley
>   of the shadow of death,
> I will fear no evil:
> For Thou art with me;
> Thy rod and Thy staff they comfort me.

Janet home again, between hospital stays. JANET FRAME

71

attracted both the very best and the very worst of reviews. Major literary figures, however, like Frank Sargeson, who reviewed it for the *New Zealand Listener*, were convinced that the book signalled the arrival of a major new talent.

Nine months later, when Janet was once again committed in Seacliff, the book may have saved her life – or, at the very least, her intellectual and artistic life. There medical staff informed her that she had been selected for a dreaded leucotomy operation (the same operation known

Just to say the words was a source of comfort, as it always had been. But this time there was more than comfort. The following morning, as if in answer to a prayer, Janet was moved back to another ward which she would always remember as 'an oasis, with its park and willow tree and its friendly ward sister'.

Soon afterwards came one of the peaks. On 4 March 1952, her sister and brother-in-law (June was now married, to Wilson Gordon) arrived at the hospital with advance copies of her first book, *The Lagoon and Other Stories*. Because of disorganisation, alcoholism and quarrels with his partners, it had taken Denis Glover five years to get the book printed, bound and published. And, published, it

TOP: **Geordie Frame, late 1940s. His almost continuous arguments with his father was one of the factors that made living at Willowglen difficult for Janet.** JANET FRAME

BOTTOM: **Janet with her one surviving sister, and her brother-in-law and nephew, Northcote, 1951: 'They enclosed one another while I stood awkwardly in the background.'** JUNE GORDON

in the United States as a lobotomy). This intervention severed the fibres connecting the front part of the brain to the rest of the cerebral cortex. Most patients who had the operation experienced a reduction in anxiety; some were rendered vegetative.

In Janet's case, momentum towards this outcome seemed unstoppable. John Money advised against it. But Lottie Frame was persuaded to give written consent. Within days of the scheduled surgery, on 26 December 1952, newspapers around the country carried a story headed 'Writer Wins Prize for Prose'. Janet had won the Hubert Church Award, New Zealand's only literary prize for fiction or non-fiction prose, for *The Lagoon*. And the Superintendent of Seacliff, Dr Geoffrey Blake-Palmer, took her off the operation list. 'I've decided that you should stay as you are. I don't want you changed.'

There was still a little over two years of intermittent hospitalisation to endure, however. It was not until 1 March 1955 that Janet finally emerged from Seacliff, discharged as a 'relieved' patient. Only now could she begin to live her life again and take control of her own affairs. She did so by deciding to move to Auckland, to live with her sister and brother-in-law on the city's North Shore. This was partly a recog-

nition that she had to avoid Willowglen if she was to stay well, and partly a wish for a wholly new start in a community where few people knew her. Being in Auckland also brought her into contact with the man who would deflect her life onto yet another direction. And this time it would be one with which she was largely in accord.

Janet's first book, *The Lagoon and Other Stories*, published six years after most of the stories were written and five years after John Money had submitted them to Denis Glover at Caxton Press. REG GRAHAM

73

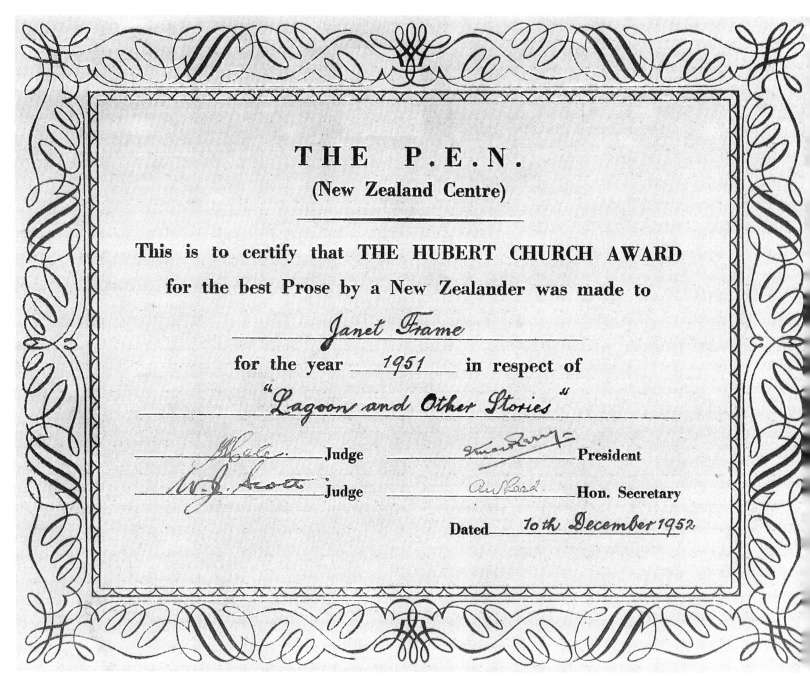

THE P.E.N.
(New Zealand Centre)

This is to certify that THE HUBERT CHURCH AWARD
for the best Prose by a New Zealander was made to

Janet Frame

for the year _1951_ in respect of

"Lagoon and Other Stories"

_____ Judge   _____ President

_____ Judge   _____ Hon. Secretary

Dated _10th December 1952_

The unexpected award for *The Lagoon and Other Stories* which saved Janet from a leucotomy in December 1952. The year specified, 1951, is an error caused by a mistaken date on the book's publication page. JANET FRAME

Her new circumstances would reveal that, far from being time wasted, Janet's associations with mental hospitals and interaction with patients there had given her an ability to burrow deep into an understanding of the human psyche, particularly the psyche of those who had been damaged or marginalised by society. And this ability would, eventually, be put to good use in her unfolding career as a writer.

Janet after her final release from Seacliff in March 1955. In her words, 'A healthy young woman with obvious false teeth, a smirking smile and a Godfrey chin.'
JANET FRAME

CHAPTER THREE INTO THE WORLD

It was a rich experience for me, to feel for the first time in my life that I was among people of my own kind.

(JANET FRAME: RADIO INTERVIEW, 11 JUNE 1976)

Frank Sargeson, gnomic doyen of the New Zealand writing community. He took Janet Frame into his household in Takapuna, Auckland, in April 1955, and created the circumstances in which she was able to write her first novel. KEVIN IRELAND

JUNE GORDON, JANET FRAME'S SISTER, HAD met the Auckland writer Frank Sargeson, who lived in a neighbouring suburb on the North Shore. He, with an interest in both Janet's talent and the circumstances in which she had begun to write, said he would like to meet her and, if possible, to help her, as he had already helped other writers.

In the last week in March 1955, therefore, the Gordons took Janet for an outing, ostensibly to explore the neighbourhood. Once they were in Takapuna it was a simple matter to suggest a visit to Sargeson's fibrolite bach, which stood behind a massive hedge on Esmonde Road. Janet remembered what transpired:

Our visit was short. What could I say? I was self-conscious, the 'funny' sister being taken for a drive. Mr Sargeson, a bearded old man [he had just turned fifty-two] in a shabby grey shirt and grey pants tied with string, smiled kindly and asked how I was, and I said nothing. He had an army hut vacant in his garden, he said. I was welcome to live and work there. I neither accepted nor refused, I was so overcome by my 'mental' status, and by seeing in person the famous writer whose anthology of New Zealand writing, *Speaking for Ourselves*, was a treasured book . . .

> 61 Gladstone Rd.,
> Northcote.
> Tuesday.
>
> Dear Frank Sargeson,
>   I thank you for
> your kind offer. I shall visit
> you one day soon; but send, in
> advance, apologies for my inclination
> to silence rather than speech.
>   You will note that
> June and Wilson have changed their
> address.
>
>   Sincerely & thanks,
>   Janet Frame.

80

He suggested that I come to see him one day, by myself . . .

'Yes,' I said shyly.

As a consequence of this invitation, Janet moved into Sargeson's army hut early in April 1955. He arranged for her to receive a medical benefit of three pounds a week, of which he was persuaded by Janet to take one pound to cover her 'keep'. From the outset, she fell into her mentor's routine life of reading and writing. They would meet for a largely silent breakfast in Sargeson's kitchen, and then go to their respective desks to spend the mornings writing, interrupted only by a cup of tea and a biscuit, which Sargeson would pass through the door of the army hut, 'averting his gaze from the nakedness of my typed pages.'

The early afternoon lunch was a more sociable affair:

Janet on the broken
steps of Sargeson's
army hut, in which she
worked and slept for
15 months in 1955
and 1956.
JANET FRAME

82

Inside the army hut: 'a bed, a built-in desk with a kerosene lamp, a rush mat on the floor . . .'
BARBARA DUGGAN

Frank would usually have a book in his hand [and] we sat facing each other with our scrambled or poached egg or cheese and rye bread, and he'd read extracts aloud and discuss the writing while I listened, accepting, believing everything he said, full of wonder at his cleverness. I worshipped him . . .

In the afternoons they read or rested, then Sargeson would go shopping in Takapuna and return to prepare the evening meal. In the latter part of the day he liked to entertain friends, many of them other writers who came to the bach for conversation and drinks and often for dinner as well. It was as a consequence of this part of the Sargeson routine that Janet met people such as Maurice and Barbara Duggan (Maurice, a

Sargeson at work in his garden behind the army hut. When Frame heard him moving about, she would type furious nonsense. Sargeson, in the midst of a writing drought, felt envious and discouraged.
CHRISTINE COLE CATLEY

short-story writer, had previously stayed in Sargeson's hut), John Reece Cole and his wife Christine, the young poet Kevin Ireland, the music teacher Jess Whitworth, and Karl and Kay Stead, who had a flat on Takapuna Beach.

At first Janet absented herself from these gatherings, then attended on the periphery as a silent listener, and then, gradually, she began to participate in the conversation and story-telling as she became comfortable in the presence of visitors. Of all of them, she was most affected by Karl and Kay Stead who, she wrote later, 'filled my life, giving me at last a place in my own years'. She remembered one evening especially:

> [They] brought two records, A Little Night Music and Beethoven's Violin Concerto played by David Oistrakh . . . I can still see that room with the bare wallboard and the wooden floor which Frank oiled each Saturday morning . . . the room that already held all the characters from *War and Peace*, *Anna Karenina*, the stories of Tolstoy and Chekhov, from Proust, Flaubert, Olive Schreiner, Doris Lessing, receiving now the music of Mozart and Beethoven while we listen. We play the record again. Karl and Frank

Karl and Kay Stead: This friendship 'filled my life giving me at last a place in my own years'. C. K. Stead

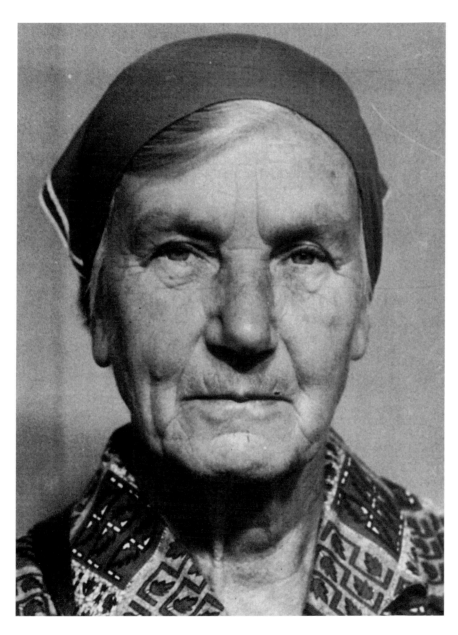

Elizabeth Pudsey
Dawson, refugee
from the English class
system: an early Frame
patron and later a close
friend.
JANET FRAME

begin to talk about Yeats. Karl reads 'Sailing to Byzantium', 'The Circus Animals' Desertion'. While I, bred on the 'old' Yeats, that is, the 'young' Yeats of 'Had I the heavens' embroidered cloths' and 'The Lake Isle of Innisfree', listen, bathed in the words and the music. I think that I recite, then, the poem I knew by heart, Dylan Thomas's 'After the Funeral', and we talk of the meaning of 'the strutting fern lay seeds on the black sill' . . .

This was bliss for Janet, the first time she had achieved intimacy with people of like mind and spirit and literary inclination. Her life would never be the same again. While there would still be phases of doubt and discouragement, she would never again have to feel wholly alone in the world. The friendships of Sargeson, the Steads, Jess Whitworth, and that of another woman to whom Sargeson would introduce her, Elizabeth Pudsey Dawson, would remain with her for as long as those people lived. And they provided a foundation on which to build other friendships, within New Zealand and abroad, in the years to come.

The *most* important product of Janet's time with Sargeson was, of course, her writing. In comparison with Sargeson, who was at that time enduring a 'dry' spell, Janet was writing a great deal, every day, within the secure structure and routine which her mentor had organised around her. By September 1955, five months after she arrived at Esmonde Road, she had completed a 64,000-word manuscript, which she initially called 'Talk of Treasure':

Pictures of great treasure in the midst of sadness and waste haunted me and I [had begun] to think, in fiction, of a child-hood, home life, hospital life, using people known to me as a base for the main characters, and inventing minor characters. For [the central character] Daphne I chose a sensitive, poetic, frail person, who (I hoped) would give depth to inner worlds and perhaps a clearer, at least an individual, perception of outer worlds. The other characters, similarly fictional, were used to portray aspects of my 'message' – the excessively material outlook of 'Chicks', the confusion of Toby, the earthy make-up of Francie, and the toiling parents, the nearest characters to my own parents. The setting was W, a small town which the publisher later named Waimaru [a conflation of Waitaki and Oamaru] . . .

The Manager,
Pegasus Press,
Oxford Terrace,
Christchurch.

Dear Sir,

I have written a prose work of approximately sixty-five thousand words, and wonder if you would consider reading it please. If it were up to standard , maybe it could be published though I understand publishing in New Zealand is in a bad way at present. Shall I send it to you? I should like this communication to be completely confidential, and enclose a stamped addressed envelope for your reply.

Thank you.

Janet Frame.

Pub marked 16 Sept. *Recd 14 Sept. AW*

Janet's tentative letter of inquiry to Pegasus Press about her first novel, then called 'Talk of Treasure'. Its date of reception is noted and initialled by **Albion Wright.** CANTERBURY MUSEUM

MEMORANDUM OF AGREEMENT

Made this day of   **Thursday, November 17**   19~~5~~5 .

between   JANET FRAME

of   14 Esmond Road, Takapuna, Auckland, New Zealand

(hereinafter called the Author, which expression, wherever the context admits, shall include the Author's executors, administrators and assigns) on the one part, and PEGASUS PRESS LIMITED 14 Oxford Terrace, Christchurch (hereinafter called the Publisher, which expression, wherever the context admits, shall include the Publisher's executors, administrators and assigns, or successors in business as the case may be) on the other part, whereas the author has written, compiled or edited a literary work at present entitled

"Talk of Treasure"

consisting of 75,000   words or thereabouts, it is mutually agreed between the parties as follows:

1.   The Author undertakes to deliver the manuscript of the work typed and ready for the printer by November 20, 1955, and the Publisher shall, unless prevented by war, strikes, lock-outs or other circumstances beyond the Publisher's control, within   **twelve**   months of the delivery of the complete manuscript, unless otherwise mutually agreed, at his own risk and expense produce and publish the work.

Should the Author neglect to deliver the manuscript by the prescribed date the Publisher may, if he thinks fit, decline to publish the work, in which case this Agreement will be annulled subject to the proviso that the Author shall not be at liberty to publish the work elsewhere without first offering it to the Publisher on the terms of this Agreement.

The Author undertakes to read and correct his proofs and to return them to the Publisher within ten days of their receipt.

2.   The Author hereby warrants to the Publisher that the said work is in no way whatever a violation of any existing copyright and that it contains nothing obscene, indecent, or (with the intention of the Author) libellous, and will indemnify the Publisher against any loss, injury or damage, including any legal costs or expenses properly occasioned to, or incurred by, the Publisher in consequence of any breach (unknown to the Publisher) of this warranty.

3.   The copyright in the work shall remain the property of the Author, but in consideration of the payments hereinafter mentioned, the sole and exclusive right to produce or reproduce the work or any abridgment of the work or any substantial part of the work in any form for the period of unrestricted copyright is hereby vested in the Publisher throughout the world.

The first page of Frame's first publishing contract, with Pegasus Press.
CANTERBURY MUSEUM

At Sargeson's suggestion, Janet did not send the manuscript to Caxton Press, because it was no longer at the forefront of New Zealand literary publishing. She posted it instead to Albion Wright at Pegasus Press, which was also located in Christchurch and which had picked up many of the writers formerly in the Caxton stable (Allen Curnow, Denis Glover, James K. Baxter, for example). To Sargeson's surprise, Albion Wright accepted it at once and Janet signed her first publisher's contract dated 17 November (she had never been offered one for *The Lagoon and Other Stories*). Unhappy with the title, however, Wright changed it to *Owls Do Cry*, the phrase taken from Janet's frontispiece quotation from *The Tempest*:

Where the bee sucks, there suck I;
In a cowslip's bell I lie;
There I couch when owls do cry;
On the bat's wing I do fly . . .

With Janet's career as a novelist apparently launched, and celebrated, Sargeson set to work to implement the second stage of his plan for his protégée. He had decided that she needed what he himself had sought at a younger age, and what he believed *all* New Zealand writers should have as a context within which to view their own country: overseas experience. And he set to work to raise, from public and private sources, sufficient money for Janet to buy a sea passage to London.

Sargeson had an additional reason for wanting Janet to move on, however. While deeply committed to her and her welfare (indeed, he told his correspondents that he 'loved' her), he was finding caring for her without remission a strain. 'I think I could have put up with the burden if Janet had been prepared to find three or four people about New Zealand to whom she could have gone . . . in rotation (including myself, of course),' he told E. P. Dawson. In fact, part of the strain was self-inflicted. When Sargeson had got around to asking Janet *why* she had been sent to hospital, she had told him she was schizophrenic, which was what she believed at the time. Sargeson had then done precisely what Janet herself had done a decade earlier: he sought out reference books on the nature of schizophrenia and was horrified by what he read.

He believed, from that point, that there was a real chance that if Janet became excessively distressed, she might murder him in his bed. He even told people that this was a possibility, and that it alarmed him. That worry, and Janet's own occasional annoyance at feeling so

Albion Wright, Janet's
New Zealand publisher
for fifteen years –
a dashing, flamboyant
and not terribly
meticulous man.
PEGASUS PRESS

Dear Mr. Sargeson,

Miss Frame has asked me to write you a chaste courteous note to say she prefers not to have her warrants posted. If she finds herself penniless before her return to Takapuna this Saturday, I have suggested she help herself to my own illimitable and, to be quite frank, mysterious income.

I must say that I hesitate to compare Charlotte Brontë's letters to her publishers with my own proposed note to the C. Press. My note to Miss Brontë would seem as offending in delicacy as a potato cooked with an eye in it. I shall however write the note as you bid, being the daughter of a different & more daring age and also

your faithful Secretary,
Aphrodite Taillefer Thickpenny

One of the dozens of playful notes Janet would write to Frank Sargeson in the course of her stay at Esmonde Road. ALEXANDER TURNBULL LIBRARY

much of her life organised for her (as it had been in hospital), created some stress between them. There were days when they didn't communicate.

The situation was resolved in May 1956 by news that the State Literary Fund had awarded Janet £300 to allow her to travel to Europe, experience European culture, and live and write there. The fare would cost £125, the remainder would support her and help pay for further travel. Sargeson also persuaded poet and *Landfall* editor Charles Brasch, and E. P. Dawson, with whom Janet was staying in Mt Maunganui when she heard of the Literary Fund's decision, to contribute additional money in support of her quest.

It took Janet two further months to make her plans, buy her ticket, pack her belongings, and make arrangements for the proofreading and production of *Owls Do Cry* (which would appear in April 1957). On 31 July 1956 she sailed out of Wellington Harbour on the *Ruahine*, on which she had booked a berth in a six-berth cabin. After four weeks, most of which Janet spent in the ship's hospital suffering from the combined effects of seasickness and influenza, the vessel docked at Southampton and Janet boarded the train for Waterloo

Station, London. What she conceived of as her Great Adventure was about to begin . . .

It did not begin well, however. On Jess Whitworth's advice, her intention was to base herself initially at the Society of Friends Hostel in Euston Road, to which she had written ahead to reserve a room. Then she would take cheaper

Janet Frame's first passport photograph, June 1956. In Sargeson's words, 'a fresh-complexioned Scottish type with reddish hair . . . and quite athletic'. ALEXANDER TURNBULL LIBRARY

Janet at sea at last, heading for Europe.
JANET FRAME

First footfall in a foreign
land: in merciless heat
at **Willemstad, Curaçao.**
JANET FRAME

accommodation in a 'garden room' in Clapham, also recommended by Whitworth, for a longer period. From that base she would find a job that would allow her to support herself and accumulate further savings. Then, as the weather became colder, she would head south for Ibiza, one of the Balearic Islands off the coast of Spain, which friends of Sargeson had recommended as a cheap, safe and pleasant place in which to live.

Janet tripped, however, on the very first step in this tightly choreographed plan. The Friends Hostel had no record of her booking. Her shock and momentary panic that this should be so was mitigated by the writer in her detecting at once the mythological and artistic implications of such a setback:

> I felt . . . the perennial drama of the Arrival and its place in myth and fiction, and I again experienced the thrilling sense of being myself excavated as reality, the ore of the polished fiction. The journey, the arrival, the surprises and problems of arrival . . . For a moment the loss of the letter . . . seemed to be unimportant beside the fictional gift of the loss, as if within every event lay a reflection reached only through the

imagination and its various servant languages, as if like the shadows in Plato's cave, our lives and the world contain mirror cities revealed to us by our imagination.

The gift of this insight did not eliminate the need to find accommodation on a dreary autumn day in London, however. On the advice of the hostel receptionist, Janet took a taxi to the YWCA in Bloomsbury. There, she found, she could share a room for two nights with a woman from Singapore. She also discovered a second insight which, even though it was early days, gave special significance to her journey. She was experiencing a sense of liberty and independence which she had never felt in New Zealand, where she was always likely to encounter reminders of family, friendships or her time in hospitals. In London she had no 'personal history'. There was no one there likely to recognise Janet Frame or know about her time in Seacliff. With this realisation came the lifting of an enormous weight. She told Sargeson by letter that, not only was she surviving, she had 'never felt more free'. And that was a feeling that was to intensify as the days and weeks in London progressed.

From the YWCA Janet rang the number Jess

Whitworth had given her for the 'garden room' in Clapham. An Irishman answered and told her that he had authority to let rooms in the absence of the owners. The following day Janet took her luggage in a taxi to Cedars Road and was installed by Patrick Reilly in a small damp-smelling room behind a large Victorian brick house. The room contained a bed, a wardrobe, a chair, an electric plate connected to a meter, and an assortment of dishes, pots and pans.

'Patrick Reilly', the dense, dull, moralistic Irishman who would take Frame into his care and dog her years in London. MICHAEL KING

Reilly fetched a table from the cellar so that Janet could use her typewriter. She was to share the bathroom and lavatory in the main house.

By New Zealand criteria, the room was little more than a garden shed and represented the lowest possible standard of accommodation. By London standards it was cheap and adequate. Frame took it, and she accepted the fussy attentions of Patrick Reilly – 'dependable, self-satisfied, bigoted, lonely, religious' – because she had no other friend in the city. She used 4 Cedars Road initially as a base from which to explore the rest of London. She gazed over the city from Hampstead Heath and experienced both positive and negative feelings about her own discovery of the Old World:

> How different it appeared to be in New
> Zealand where the place names and the
> landscape, the trees, the sea and the sky
> still echoed with their first voice while
> the earliest works of art uttered their
> response, in a primary dialogue with
> the Gods . . . I did not know whether to
> thank or curse John Keats and others
> for having planted their sedge, basil,
> woodbine and nodding violets, and
> arranged their perennial nightingales to
> sing in my mind . . . That evening in my

Garden Room I read and recited Keats and others . . . having followed the advice of Jess Whitworth and joined the local Clapham Library.

Janet spent the rest of September sightseeing and writing. She sent some poems to John Lehmann at *London Magazine*, and he returned them with the comment that they did not quite come up to the standard of English required. She accepted invitations to go out on dates with a physics teacher who lived in the main house and with a Nigerian student called Clement Nweze. These encounters did not lead to enduring friendships. And she visited a household of would-be writers and artists whose address had been supplied by friends of Sargeson. Here she met David Kozubei, a poet of Polish-Jewish descent, with whom she would remain in contact for some years.

Early in October 1956 Janet booked her European travel to the Spanish island of Ibiza. Then she took a job for the rest of the month as a housemaid-waitress at the Battersea Polytechnic Hostel, working from six o'clock in the morning until noon. Very much aware of the temperature dropping and the days shortening, she used her afternoons to write and to prepare for her removal to the 'warm south'. On 30 October, Patrick Reilly farewelled her at Waterloo Station and asked her to stay 'fancy free'. By late afternoon the following day she was in Paris. And three days later, after a further journey by train and ferry, she landed in Ibiza. She was by this time without all luggage except her handbag because, as she left Paris, she had mistaken the 'left luggage' counter for the 'consignment' one. The missing bags would take weeks to catch up with her.

Ibiza at this time was a town of 12,000 people on the island of the same name. Over millennia it had been occupied successively by Phoenicians, Egyptians, Greeks, Romans, Carthaginians, Arabs and Catalans, all of whom had left an imprint on the island's culture and architecture. Earlier New Zealand visitors, who had included the artists Frances Hodgkins, Maud Burge and Douglas Glass, were impressed by the 'intense light reflecting off the pale rocky earth and the whitewashed houses'. Janet had been persuaded to move there because of the extraordinarily cheap cost of living outside the summer holiday season. There was virtually no cash economy on the island at this time and anyone with money – especially pounds, dollars, francs or marks – was wealthy by local standards. Janet planned to stay there from four to six months.

Ibiza in the Balearic Islands, which Janet would come to remember, literally and metaphorically, as a 'mirror city'. GIL HANLY

She spent her first night in a cheap hotel and went wandering the next morning. She walked through the old city with its remains of Roman walls, and up to the top of a hill, from where she could see fields and olive groves running down to the sea on the other side of the island:

> I sat leaning against a grey rock that was massed like an accumulation of layers and layers of ancient olive leaves. I shared the solitude with a small herd of wild goats, and the silence with the distant sounds of the fishing boats. The greyleaved olive trees with their twisted branches and trunks turned in defiance of the sea wind, and the white-grey stones like long-fallen snow that had refused to melt on the red soil beneath the trees, drew from me a feeling of tenderness, as if this land were mine and I had known it long ago. It was, of course, Shelley's world, and I *had* known it in poetry . . . I was happy just to *be* where I had always felt most at home – outside, under the sky, on a hilltop overlooking the ocean.

That same morning Janet encountered two middle-aged women, dressed in black and gathering firewood. She used her Catalan phrase-book to convey the information that she was a writer, not a tourist, looking for somewhere cheap to live and work. The women became excited and explained in a mixture of Spanish, French and sign language that the house of their *patron* was in the town and available for rent, and that they would take her there. He was living off the island and the house was in the care of his brother, Fermin.

When Janet saw the house she could scarcely believe her good fortune. It had a spacious bedroom where she could work and sleep. There was a kitchen with a wood range and a lavatory. All this (and, she believed, the rest of the house) she could have for ten pesetas – about two shillings – a day. The two servants who had brought her there, Catalina and Francesca, lived next door but would use the kitchen for preparing meals. And the owner's son would from time to time practise his violin playing. These three visitors, and Fermin, would help her with Spanish conversation and local information. Within days Janet was writing to Sargeson and John Money about how well she had settled in and how happy she was. Her lost luggage, including her typewriter, turned up before Christmas.

Almost at once Janet was back to writing. Before her typewriter arrived, she hand-wrote

An Ibiza street: harsh
white light and a sense
of antiquity.
GIL HANLY

poems and stories. After Christmas she set to work in earnest on a new novel, tentatively titled 'Uncle Pylades' (son of the Phocian king Stophius and husband of Electra). By the end of January she had typed 50,000 words of this manuscript. She also reported how free she felt, to be (as in London) in a place where people had no knowledge of her past:

> . . . I had never felt so much at home. I rejoiced that I was alone on a Mediterranean island, speaking no English, with my Spanish welcomed as my English never had been, for my struggle to express my thoughts was attended by the kindness of those who were proud that I was trying to speak their language and who were eager to explain, suggest, help, and teach, whereas in speaking one's native language to others who also speak it one is alone, struggling to meet the expectations of the listener.

The idyll in which Janet found herself was violated in late January 1957 when she discovered that she was required to share the house with an American artist named Harvey Cohen. He too was taken aback to find another lodger there. Eventually, however, the two foreigners established a harmonious routine whereby they used the kitchen at different times, worked alone throughout the day, and occasionally shared meals at night. He was genial and, an artist himself, he understood the conditions Janet needed so as to be able to work.

The real interruption to her routine occurred in February when Cohen brought a friend to the house one night, a fellow American named George Parlette. Parlette was an accountant, originally from Ohio but most recently living in Switzerland, where he had a wife and two children. He omitted to tell Janet about his marriage; and he said he was a college professor who wrote poetry. He also claimed to be the same age as her, thirty-two, when he was in fact two years her junior. She was charmed and flattered by his attentions and saw in them an opportunity to fill a major gap in her experience. A week later she wrote to Sargeson about her change of circumstance:

> [Work] is not going very well – I'm leaving it in my unconscious while I have some human experience . . . a love affair with a friend of Harvey's . . . We've got to the slightly jealous stage now, where he makes references to 'all the men you've known' and I refer to 'all your women' . . . The whole thing is very fascinating . . .

[We] have taken to going [for] long cycle rides around the island . . . then return to the city at nightfall, then wine and dine, then go to his house, and go to bed, which occupation I like very much, it being more comforting than a hotwater bottle, for a hotwater bottle gets cold in the middle of the night, but a man stays warm at night, and in the morning is sometimes very hot.

The whole affair lasted little more than a fortnight. And, as Janet acknowledged, was dependent on mutual dishonesty: he misled her about his age, occupation and marital status; she misled him about her record of sexual inexperience and the quality of the execrable poetry he was writing for her. Such dishonesty had to be tolerated, however, to ensure that the encounter took place and gave her the opportunity to taste and evaluate it, when she had never before had such an opportunity. The experience left her with the conviction that, in addition to compatibility, the major ingredient of any future relationship had to be absolute honesty. It also left her pregnant.

The prospect of pregnancy and having to give birth as a solo mother soured for Janet the experience of living in Ibiza. The people there

who had been so kind to her would, she believed, be horrified and disillusioned in their view of her. Rather than put these fears to the test, she decided in late March 1957 to relocate herself to Andorra, where she knew nobody and where, she believed, her money would go even further than it would in Ibiza.

And so she said farewell to her Ibizian friends and travelled by ferry to Barcelona and on to Andorra by taxi (by this time so much snow had fallen in the Pyrenees that the roads were impassable for buses). There, in the town of Les Escaldes, she found board with an impoverished couple who had two children and another lodger, El Botti Mario, an Italian who worked as a guide and a smuggler during the winter months and picked grapes in the South of France in autumn. She wrote to a friend:

My room faces directly on to a mountain. At first, snow-covered, but the snow is gradually vanishing on the upper slopes; higher in the Pyrenees it seems to be always snowing . . . In my walks I stumble over violets, but their smell seems frozen inside them. The valley is full of trees, poplars and larches and pines . . . I do my washing in the communal washing trough . . . supplied with water from the

Les Escaldes, Andorra, where Janet lodged with an impoverished family and suffered a miscarriage in 1957.
JANET FRAME

hot mountain springs . . . [Life] is dearer here than in Ibiza.

One reason for the walks was that Janet was taking quinine tablets, then rushing up and down mountain paths and plunging into hot springs in an attempt to dislodge the foetus in her womb. The measures succeeded and one night she miscarried when she attempted to change a light bulb. 'I did not realise until the baby was born that I had accepted it and was preparing for it. I knew a feeling that was stronger than regret but not as intense as a bereavement, a no-woman's land of feeling where a marvellous sense of freedom sprang up beside hate for myself.'

No sooner was she released from one threat, however, than she found herself trapped in another. El Botti Mario, her fellow lodger, had pounced on her one day and, when repulsed, was so impressed by her virtue that he proposed marriage, even though it was a mere four weeks since they had met. By refusing to answer one way or the other, and by not saying an unequivocal no, Janet gave the impression that she had agreed. And so, in the eyes of the rest of the household and those of the immediate community, they were engaged. The only way to escape this potential prison, Janet decided, was to run away.

And so she told her fiancé that she had things to see to in England. Then she bought a round-trip ticket to London after being assured that she would get a refund if she failed to use the return portion. She notified Patrick Reilly of her arrival and he was waiting to meet her at Waterloo. After the vicissitudes surrounding her relationships with George Parlette and El Botti Mario, the company of Patrick Reilly seemed the lesser of many other possible evils. He, meanwhile, had changed lodgings, to a

El Botti Mario, the Italian to whom Janet became engaged in Andorra: 'a spiv, a lounge lizard, and possibly a gangster.' JANET FRAME

One of the alpine valleys in Andorra where Janet would 'walk out' with her fiancé. JANET FRAME

house in Clapham Common South. And he had taken the liberty of accepting a room there for Janet and paying her first week's rent.

Apart from the emotional consequences of the miscarriage, the unexpected but temporary appearance in London of her brother Geordie, and the cloying attentions of Patrick Reilly, the most acute source of stress Janet faced back in London in May 1957 was a lack of money. *Owls Do Cry* had been published to generally good reviews in New Zealand in April 1957. But it was to be more than a year before any money from Pegasus Press found its way to her. She was insufficiently pleased with the new manuscript, 'Uncle Pylades', to offer it to anybody. So she took a job as an usher at a local cinema to give herself the means to pay rent at the new house, which was more expensive than the 'garden flat' at Cedars Rd.

After four weeks, however, monetary contributions from E. P. Dawson and John Money allowed her to relinquish the job and return to writing. In July she decided to find an agent, with a view to getting *Owls Do Cry*

Covers designed for the New Zealand edition of *Owls Do Cry*, **published the week Janet suffered her miscarriage on the other side of the world. That depicting the main street of a provincial New Zealand town at night was the one chosen.**
CANTERBURY MUSEUM

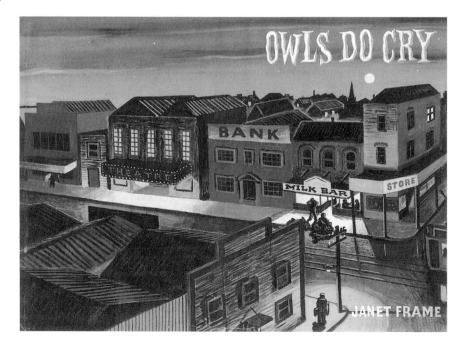

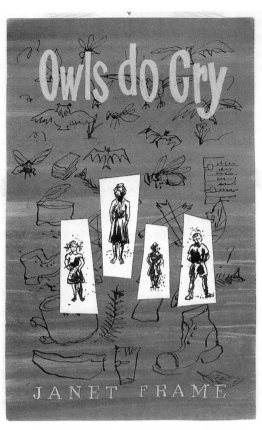

(and future work) published in markets outside New Zealand. She selected A. M. Heath Ltd at random from the *Artists' and Writers' Yearbook*. It was a lucky choice. Patience Ross, the A. M. Heath partner who interviewed her, was one of the most admired and successful agents in the United Kingdom. She was also a lesbian who had suffered from clinical depression. These latter circumstances meant that she viewed herself as someone who lived on the margins of society. She was immensely interested in and sympathetic to Janet's history, and she admired *Owls Do Cry*. She agreed to take her on as a client and to seek publishers for her first novel and for new work in London and New York, where A. M. Heath used the respected literary agency Brandt and Brandt.

Janet left Ross's office feeling, for the first time, optimistic about her chances of publication in England, though her new writing was not going well. That same month she took her first major trip out of London into the English and Welsh countryside. She visted Gene Beach, formerly a nurse at Seacliff, at her home in Cardiff. Less than a week later, she walked from Clapham South to Denmark Hill for an interview at the Maudsley Hospital, which had a worldwide reputation for enlightened treatment of psychiatric patients.

The visit to the Maudsley came about as a consequence of a renewed correspondence with John Money. He, alarmed about the effects of the miscarriage (which he believed had been an abortion), and mistaking one of Janet's 'metaphorical' letters for evidence of hallucinations, recommended that she visit Dr Michael Shepherd. Frame herself, depressed that her writing was not going well and believing that

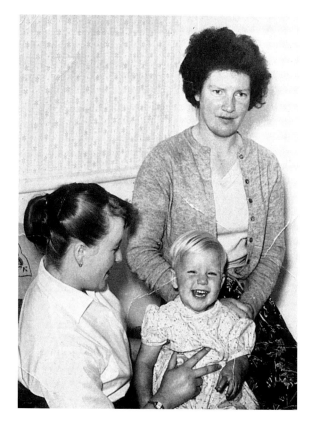

Shortly before entering the Maudsley Hospital, Janet visits Gene Beach who, as Nurse 'Taffy', had befriended her at Seacliff. GENE BEACH

she still had the sentence of schizophrenia hanging over her, felt disposed to seek medical help. The result of her consultation with Shepherd was that on 19 August 1957 she became a voluntary patient at the Maudsley Hospital.

She remained there, on this occasion, for six months. The treatment was a familiar Maudsley smorgasbord of 'supportive and re-educational' talks with a psychiatrist, a young American by the name of Alan D. Miller, some occupational therapy (writing and painting), and the 'support, safety and understanding' of nursing staff, who were present in far larger numbers than they had ever been in the course of Janet's hospitalisations in New Zealand. Her hospital notes showed that, over the time she was there, Janet's episodes of withdrawal and depression recurred, but with less frequency and intensity. Most importantly, the hospital's consultants told her that she was not and never had been schizophrenic. At the time of her discharge in January 1958, she was judged to have had 'a pathological personality with schizoid and depressive features, and difficulties in ordering perceptions and controlling behaviour'.

On leaving hospital, the first decision she made was to get as far away as possible from Patrick Reilly. The most unpleasant parts of her sojourn at the Maudsley had been the visits which he had used as an opportunity to sermonise about her plight and what he viewed as the moral degeneracy of her occupation. She abandoned Clapham for Kentish Town and took a damp basement flat in Fortess Road. That proved unsatisfactory and she moved across the street to a flat above a shop, which she shared with three other women, one of them a librarian, Mildred Surry, who would become a friend.

John Money in the United States, mid-1950s. It was his letter of referral that sent Frame to the Maudsley Hospital in July 1957. Janet Frame

109

The Maudsley, an oasis of good practice in an impoverished sector of medicine.
R. H. Cawley

Janet tried to resume a writing routine in the hours that her flatmates were away at their jobs, and initially she focused on poetry. She also renewed her acquaintance with David Kozubei, which led to her becoming sexually involved with an artist friend of his. With these two men, she began to spend increasing amounts of time, at the expense of her writing, hanging out at Soho cafés with unemployed painters and poets.

On 22 May 1958, fearing that *Owls Do Cry* might after all appear in London under the name of Janet Frame, she went to a lawyer and changed her name to Nene Janet Paterson Clutha: Nene in admiration for the

Maori chief Tamati Waka Nene and because she had been called Nini as a child; Paterson for her Scottish grandmother; and Clutha for the mighty river of that name back home which sliced through Central Otago. In future she was to write as Janet Frame but *live* as Janet Clutha.

Part of her rehabilitation was attributable to her weekly visits to the Maudsley and continuing talks with Alan Miller. In June 1958, however, Miller returned to the United States and Janet panicked about what she imagined would be her inability to cope without his presence and his help. As she had done previously, she descended into a spiral of anxiety and confusion in which she was unable to write or to live happily. When an attempt to re-enter the Maudsley failed, Janet rang the hospital one night from a public telephone near Waterloo Bridge and announced that she intended to throw herself into the Thames. Police were sent to collect her and bring her to the Maudsley. This time she was admitted again as a voluntary patient. And this time too she would meet the man who would do more than any other person to help her re-establish a sense of equilibrium in her life and work.

Robert Hugh Cawley, the consulting psychiatrist assigned to Frame in September 1958,

was, at thirty-four, an exact contemporary of his patient. But he had a far wider experience of scholarship and of human behaviour than might have been expected of a man of his age. Before studying psychiatry he had taken degrees in zoology and medical statistics. In addition, as a student at Birmingham University, he had edited the student paper and a literary journal. Janet found him approachable (despite his voice), erudite, conscientious, courteous and easy to talk to. He found this particular patient 'rather anxious and unhappy. She was a bit perplexed and not always able to express her thoughts and feelings in anything more than brief sentences and phrases.' He agreed that she needed access to the healing processes that the Maudsley had to offer.

And so, once again, Janet was absorbed back into the environment that she had found so helpful at the time of her first admission. This gave her respite from apprehension, support during periods of depression, exposure to the 'therapeutic community' of nursing and ward staff, and – most important of all – access to Dr Cawley several times a week for what she came to call 'an accounting process – an examination of emotional, personal, and even financial budget with a view to balancing all so that I could survive . . .'

As before, improvements in Janet's condition were incremental rather than dramatic. But, after nine months, Cawley had convinced her that 'I was myself, I was an adult, I need not explain myself to others. The "you should" days were over.' He also convinced her that 'I genuinely needed to write, that it was a way of life for me, and that the best practical help . . . was to arrange a National Assistance weekly payment and for me to find accommodation near the hospital so that we might continue our talks'.

It was this strategy, and Janet's conviction of its merit, that allowed her to leave the Maudsley on 12 June 1959. She had arranged to rent a room in which to live and write in the adjacent suburb of Camberwell, which had formerly been the home of John Ruskin, Robert Browning and Felix Mendelssohn. And she was booked to attend weekly sessions at the hospital with Cawley. This time, she wrote to Sargeson, she planned to 'write like hell'. And this time she was right.

Robert Cawley, the Maudsley psychiatrist who persuaded Frame to meet her own expectations rather than those of others; and who would become, in time, her beloved RHC, to whom she would dedicate seven books. R. H. CAWLEY

THE BETHLEM ROYAL HOSPITAL
AND THE MAUDSLEY HOSPITAL

Patron: H.R.H. PRINCESS ALEXANDRA, G.C.V.O.

Chairman
SIR ALAN WILSON, F.R.S.,

House Governor and Secretary:
L. H. W. PAINE, M.A.

Telephone:
01-703 6333

Telegraphic Address:
MAUDSLEY LONDON
SE5

THE MAUDSLEY HOSPITAL   DENMARK HILL   LONDON SE5 8AZ

<u>To whom it may concern</u>

Miss Janet Frame Clutha has told me that a number of literary
scholars and editors of anthologies are publishing biographical comments
which refer to her previous state of mind as sick or disordered. I
understand that some people are going so far as to suggest that her
creative ability is in some way related to a history of mental illness.

Miss Clutha was under my care between 1958 and 1963, and I saw
her frequently during that time; she and others have kept me informed
about her activities since then. She has been seen by a number of
eminent psychiatrists, all of whom agree with my opinion that she has
never suffered from a mental illness in any formal sense. She went
through a long period of considerable unhappiness before making various
decisions about how to spend her life.

I have told Miss Clutha that in my opinion any writer who publishes
comments referring to her "disordered mind" or "mental illness" is running
two risks. One is of public ridicule at the hands of scholars more
knowledgeable and informed about these matters. The other is litigation.

R.H. Cawley, PhD, MRCP, FRCPsych.
Physician.

20th April 1974

Letter from Bob Cawley testifying that Janet had 'never suffered from a mental illness'. She would use this document to caution scholars who alleged that her genius was the product of a disordered mind.
JANET FRAME

113

CHAPTER FOUR THE LIFE OF A WRITER

Writing is a boon, analgesic and so on. I think it's all that matters to me. I dread emerging from it each day.

(JANET FRAME TO FRANK SARGESON, NOVEMBER 1978)

The whitewashed house in Grove Hill Road, Camberwell, where Frame would live for three years and consolidate both her career and her reputation as a writer. MICHAEL KING

JANET FRAME BEGAN WHAT WOULD PROVE TO be an uninterrupted life as a writer at Grove Hill Road, Camberwell, London. Over the next three years, from mid-1959 to mid-1962, she would write three new novels and two volumes of short stories. And her first novel, *Owls Do Cry*, would be published in Britain and the United States. She began to attract the reputation that would eventually place her in the company of the great writers of the twentieth century.

While Janet was in the Maudsley, *Owls Do Cry* had been launched on the rounds of British and American publishers by Patience Ross of A. M. Heath and Carl Brandt of Brandt and Brandt.

It was an American who bit first. George Braziller, who had established his own publishing house only four years earlier, read the New Zealand edition of the novel in one sitting in May 1959. He was hooked. '[It] was one of the most original pieces of writing that I had read in years. I immediately decided that we would publish it.' He did so in July 1960.

And it was Braziller who found the book a British publisher. Late in 1960, he recommended it to Mark Goulden, owner and managing director of W. H. Allen. Goulden, already well known for first publishing Dylan Thomas and Alan Sillitoe, gave the American edition of *Owls Do Cry* to his stepson, Jeffrey

Simmons, and Simmons advised publication. This edition appeared in London in July 1961.

Janet, meanwhile, had been hard at work on her second novel, *Faces in the Water*. The room she rented from Doris and Richard Parry, in a house shared with them, their daughter and one other boarder, had a large table that she used for eating at one end and writing at the other.

George Braziller, Janet's American publisher, who in 1960 launched what would become her international career. GEORGE BRAZILLER

I kept to the routine I began when I was living in Frank Sargeson's hut in Takapuna. I also continued the method I had adopted of buying a new school exercise book, carefully writing my name in the space provided on the cover, with the word 'Novel' in a juvenile, laborious hand beside the subject, then ruling various columns to record . . . progress, with spaces for Excuses, now called Wasted Days . . . There was more enthusiasm than usual in my working: each week [I] had an impartial observer in Dr Cawley to talk to and complain to and tell of my progress.

And it was Dr Cawley who had suggested to her the subject of this new work:

[The] story of my experiences in hospitals in New Zealand, recording faithfully every happening and the patients and staff I had known, but borrowing from what I had observed among the patients to build a more credibly 'mad' character, Istina Mavet, the narrator . . . [Planning] a subdued rather than a sensational record,

Janet's American agent Carl Brandt: young, attentive, energetic and urbane. CARL BRANDT

Mark Goulden of
W. H. Allen, the
'gambler-publisher';
and his wife Jane
who, Janet would
say, possessed
'a remarkable
resemblance to the
Queen of Spades'.
JEFFREY SIMMONS

I omitted much, aiming more for credibility than a challenge to me by those who might disbelieve my record . . .

Faces in the Water was completed in April 1960, and published in the United States in 1961 and in New Zealand and Britain in 1962. No sooner was the manuscript off her table than Janet began work on her third novel *The Edge of the Alphabet*, for which she would draw on the experience of her brother Geordie, calling the character based on him 'Toby Withers' (as she had done in *Owls Do Cry*); and on her knowledge of Patrick Reilly for the character she called 'Pat Keenan'. She finished this manuscript just before Christmas 1960.

In February 1961 she began work on a set of ideas she had been accumulating for short stories, and by April had written thirty-nine of them. Late in May 1961 she was working on her fourth novel, *Scented Gardens for the Blind*. Never before had she been able to write so continuously and so prolifically. All this new work would eventually be published, the stories in two volumes, *Snowman, Snowman* and *The Reservoir*, in 1963. *The Edge of the Alphabet* first appeared in 1962, and *Scented Gardens for the Blind* in 1963.

The equilibrium which allowed such productivity was the fruit of several features of Janet's life at this time. One was the fact that, thanks to the National Assistance organised by Bob Cawley, she had no money worries. The generally satisfactory nature of her accommodation and working conditions at Grove Hill Road provided a sense of security and continuity. And her weekly visits to Cawley at the Maudsley allowed her to dissipate anxieties well before the point at which they might have begun to cripple her. Equally important was the work routine, which she adopted with monastic dedication.

At eight o'clock . . . I turn on the radio and hear the weather forecast and the news. Then . . . I begin work for the day, sitting down at my table and my typewriter. At about half-past ten or eleven o'clock I have a break, go out and perhaps buy a *Guardian*, do some shopping . . . then come home again [and] work till lunch, when I read my paper, listen to the one o'clock news, and then begin work again . . . till half-past four when I make myself tea, which consists always of two pieces of toast, one with jam, the other with cheese . . . Of course all the time the outward things are happening I am having my inward dreams . . .

These seemingly ideal conditions persisted up till May 1962. Then, almost overnight, the situation at Grove Hill Road changed. Janet's landlord, Richard Parry, switched from a daytime to a night-time job (working as a telephonist). Now she was asked not to type or to flush the lavatory during the day, because he was sleeping. And she was unable to write at night because of the noise of television sets on the floors above and below her. These conditions and stipulations made life as a writer impossible. She was forced to move.

The cottage in Braiseworth, East Suffolk, where Janet discovered the drawbacks for a writer of country living.

JANET FRAME

122

The first alternative Janet tried, a thatched cottage in the Suffolk countryside near the village of Eye, was a disaster. She was offered a reduced rent on the condition that she be responsible for the upkeep of the cottage and its garden. These chores eventually came to absorb all her time and energy and left none for writing. She was also required to look after a dog and walk it twice a day, and this animal could not bear to let her out of its sight. 'The dog follows me everywhere,' Janet told John Money by letter. 'I can't make a move without [her] making the same move, it's uncanny . . . [even] to the lavatory and into the bathroom . . . I came here for isolation and I've never been so crowded in my life.' East Suffolk was also a long train ride away from London and her continuing weekly appointments with Bob Cawley.

Eventually, in October 1962, Janet accepted the invitation of her London publisher, Mark Goulden, to move into a flat in South Kensington. The bulk of the rent would be paid by all three of her publishers from advances to be deducted from sales of future work. From this time on, Janet would restrict her contact with the English countryside to visits to her friend E. P. Dawson, who had now returned to England from New Zealand and bought half a cottage in Norfolk.

In South Kensington, in January 1963, Janet began to work in earnest on the manuscript that would become her fifth novel, *The Adaptable Man*. The narrative of this book would show clearly the imprint of her experience in East Suffolk. But the novel as a whole had its genesis in a visit she had paid the previous year to a dentist in Camberwell:

> His consulting room looked so old and everything was frayed, and the tap was dripping in the little bowl, and it looked very sad . . . There were two things he said. He went over to the window and drew the curtain aside (it was spring) and said, 'What wouldn't I give to be in Sussex today.' He said it with such longing. And when somebody called downstairs, he said, 'Rinse whilst I'm gone' . . . It seemed like something out of the past. And so I wrote about a dentist . . . I wrote the book around him as I imagined him . . . [I] quite enjoy imagining lives for people whom I only see once or twice and don't know.

Janet's year in South Kensington was not a productive one, however. She was distracted from the novel in progress by an unfinished attempt to edit a manuscript written by a former mental hospital patient; and by bad news from home – her sole surviving sister, June Gordon, had suffered a brain haemorrhage, from which she was not, at first, expected to recover (but she did). Janet also began work on a short novel, which she called 'Towards Another Summer', and then abandoned it. It had been triggered by a poem of Charles Brasch's, her New Zealand patron, that begins:

> Always, in these islands, meeting and
>   parting
> Shake us, making tremulous the salt-
>   rimmed air . . .

and ends:

> Everywhere in light and calm the murmuring

In Norfolk: E. P. Dawson (at right) and Flint Cottage, half of which Janet would eventually inherit from her elderly friend. JANET FRAME

An indisputable success: Janet poses for photographer Jerry Bauer on the Victoria Embankment, alongside the Thames, in February 1962. JERRY BAUER

Shadow of departure; distance looks our
   way;
And none knows where he will lie down at
   night.

These preoccupations, strengthened by a visit
to the home of writer Geoffrey Moorhouse and
his New Zealand wife, provoked what Janet
called a 'roots crisis' and a period of reflection
about what exactly being a New Zealander
meant to her. That crisis was intensified by the
news in August 1963 that her father had died
in Oamaru and that she was now joint owner of
Willowglen and sole executor of her father's
estate. Janet decided to return to New Zealand
at once and, on 12 September, she sailed from
London on the return journey home. It was
a decision that in effect solved what had become an enlarging dilemma: whether to be an
English or a New Zealand writer.

Janet had left home seven years earlier as a
largely unknown would-be writer with one
book of stories to her name. She arrived in
Auckland in October 1963 as the author of four
published novels and three volumes of stories.
She had been reviewed as a matter of course
over the previous three years in quality newspapers and journals in Britain and the United
States. As she would write later, 'a dam of

opinion and speculation burst over me . . . I
[found] that I was looked on, variously, as
famous, rich, a woman of the world, sane,
insane, inevitably different from the shy unknown who had departed.'

This new-found status was reflected in the fact
that journalists boarded the ship to interview
her before she had even disembarked; and in
the number of additional requests for interviews and guest appearances that awaited her
at her sister's house on the North Shore. She
refused all such requests and, after visiting
Frank Sargeson and Jess Whitworth, headed
south to sort out her father's affairs in
Oamaru. There she was ambushed by her old
local paper, the *Oamaru Mail*, to whose children's pages she had once contributed stories
and poems.

Miss Janet Frame said she had returned
after ten years overseas [*sic*], and might
return to Oamaru to complete her
latest book, *The Adaptable Man*. Miss Frame
already has ideas for another book which
she would like to write in Oamaru. Asked
if the book would have a local setting,
[she] declined to answer. 'I lose all
enthusiasm in my writing after reading
about ideas in the Press,' she stated. 'I

Home again. Janet with her niece Pamela and the caravan in which she lived and worked while staying with the Gordons in Northcote, Auckland, October 1963. JOHN SCRIVENER

Janet and her sole surviving sister, June Gordon, in October 1963. Earlier in the year June had suffered a stroke, from which she was considered lucky to have recovered. JANET FRAME

Local girl makes good. Janet, still in her Marks and Spencer's dress, poses for the *Oamaru Mail* in the public gardens, November 1963. OAMARU MAIL

130

Willowglen after Janet had cleared out family papers and mementoes: abandoned to ruin and eventual collapse.
JANET FRAME

One of the family keepsakes that Janet saved from Willowglen: the chanter from her father's bagpipes, with which he had played his children to sleep in Glenham and Wyndham.
REG GRAHAM

generally talk trivialities and do my serious thinking when I'm writing' . . . Efforts were made to get Janet Frame to talk about herself; but this quietly spoken woman refused to be drawn.

Janet cleaned up the Willowglen house, burned items such as old clothes, broken-down appliances and papers, and saved some keepsakes for herself or other members of her family. She made the decision that she didn't want to live there – in Willowglen or in Oamaru – and she eventually gave her half-share in the property to her brother, with whom relationships were no easier than they had been before her absence abroad. She then returned to Auckland via Dunedin, where she re-established contact with Charles Brasch, who told her that he would try to secure for her a 'literary pension'; and Christchurch where, for the first time, she visited her New Zealand publisher, Albion Wright, at Pegasus Press.

Back in Auckland Janet discovered that she had been awarded a scholarship in letters by the Literary Fund. This sum, £1000, would support her fully for at least a year. And so she established herself in a flat in Devonport on the city's North Shore and resumed writing. Her first piece was an essay for 'Beginnings', a series in which writers explained how they came to be writers, which Charles Brasch planned to run in his journal *Landfall*.

In this essay Janet wrote about the near-Gothic quality of her early family life ('a background of poverty, drunkenness, attempted murder and near-madness'); and about the supposed relationship of her writing to her hospitalisation ('I knew . . . that unless I devoted my time wholly to making designs from my dreams . . . I should spend the remainder of my life in hospital'). She made these points because Charles Brasch had indicated that the case for a literary pension would be strengthened by evidence of a disadvantaged background. Over the years, however, she came to regret the way in which journalists and critics would ransack the 'Beginnings' essay to support the 'insane writer' scenario, and to hypothesise about which members of her family might be drunkards, murderers and lunatics.

In April 1964 Janet left Devonport in favour of a bach on Waiheke Island, a subtropical outpost of Auckland that lies on the Hauraki Gulf ten miles east of the city. Here, at last, she managed to complete *The Adaptable Man* (it would be published the following year). And she wrote most of another novel, her sixth,

In Vital Books, Auckland, with veteran politician-writer John A. Lee, the bookshop's owner. JANET FRAME

LEFT: Janet pays her first visit to her New Zealand publisher and is photographed smiling shyly at the door by Albion Wright. Deluged by his charm, she found herself unable to discuss points of their business relationship with which she was unhappy. PEGASUS PRESS

titled *A State of Siege*, about a lone woman living in circumstances very much like those in which Janet found herself on the island (and, indeed, the narrative was closely based on the life of a schoolteacher, Rebe Rowlandson, who had been an earlier owner and occupant of the same bach).

She returned to Auckland in September, where she required an operation to remove a tumour from one of her breasts, a recurrence of an earlier growth. She came out of the anaesthetic to learn that the tumour, like its predecessor, was benign; and to hear that she had been awarded the Burns Fellowship at Otago University, a position for which she had not even applied. She decided to accept the fellowship, which would mean a return to the city of her birth and of her teacher training. But first she determined to make a quick trip to the United States, to visit John Money in Baltimore and her American publisher, George Braziller, in New York; and to go on to England to 'settle her affairs' there, see her UK publisher and agent, and to travel to Norfolk to visit E. P. Dawson, who had recently told Janet that she was to be the executor and benficiary of the older woman's will.

Janet arrived in Dunedin for the third time in her life in January 1965. She was to remain there for the next seven years, a choice that would confirm her decision to be a writer who lived and worked in New Zealand. In that first year, the year of her fellowship, she completed *A State of Siege* and began a new novel, which would be published in British and New Zealand editions as *The Rainbirds*, and in the United States as *Yellow Flowers in the Antipodean Room*. She also made a selection of the stories published in the United States as *The Reservoir* and *Snowman Snowman* for a new single volume edition, *The Reservoir and other stories*, to be published in New Zealand and the United Kingdom in 1966.

Several other things occurred which had the effect of further bonding Janet to Dunedin. She renewed friendships with Charles Brasch, and with the librarian Dorothy Neal White, who had been on the staff at Dunedin Teachers' Training College and had visited her in Seacliff Hospital. She formed close associations with the poet Ruth Dallas and the non-fiction writer Dennis McEldowney. In 1966, she was succeeded as Burns Fellow by the poet James K. Baxter and, in the course of that year, she developed close friendships with him, his wife Jacquie, and their children Hilary and John.

At the close of 1965, thanks to an additional grant of 'surplus' Burns Fellowship funds, Janet was able to buy the first house she had ever owned entirely on her own. It was a late nineteenth-century workman's cottage in Opoho, high in the hills above Dunedin's North-East Valley. Up there, she would write, an 'immense sky sprawled above the hills, with every cloud going somewhere in a tail of white or black smoke, pursued by storm and wind and sun'. This house was to be an anchor for her life and career in the coming years; and its equity would eventually provide her with the means to buy other houses in other parts of the country.

It was from Dunedin in 1967 that Janet began to make a series of pilgrimages to writers' and artists' colonies in the United States. She visited Yaddo in upstate New York for the first time in 1967, and subsequently in 1969, 1970

The first house Janet Frame owned, at 61 Evans St, Opoho. This property, bought with Burns Fellowship money, gave her an anchor to New Zealand, and a base in Dunedin for seven years. JANET FRAME

On the Otago Peninsula in May 1966, at Charles Brasch's crib: (from left) Brasch, Karl Stead and Frame.
RUTH DALLAS

With Dunedin friends, 1966: Frame, poet James K. Baxter, painter Michael Illingworth, Dene Illingworth, Jacquie Baxter, John Baxter. JOHN MONEY

The Mansion at Yaddo, Saratoga Springs, where Janet periodically lived and worked with American artists and writers from 1967 to 1982. It was here that she met her friend and patron John Marquand.
JANET FRAME

and 1971. In the course of those visits she wrote the novels that eventually emerged as *Intensive Care* and *Daughter Buffalo*, and the children's book *Mona Minum and the Smell of the Sun*. Her one volume of poems, *The Pocket Mirror*, first appeared in 1967 in the United States when she was there; but most of them had been written in Dunedin. In 1969 too she had a spell at the MacDowell colony in New Hampshire.

Janet at the Yaddo pool table, a scene that would have surprised her friends and family in New Zealand.
ALEXANDER TURNBULL LIBRARY

The boat landing at Salt Cay, the 'Treasure Island' in the Bahamas on which Janet spent two holidays with the Marquands and their wealthy relations. JANET FRAME

Subsequently Janet was to describe these working sojourns in the company of other writers, and of musicians and artists, as 'rich experiences'. The colonies provided what was for her a series of perfect working environments – quiet studio space for composition, access to good libraries, and the company of like-minded people for the evening periods of recreation. Janet also made friendships there, some of which would be lifelong.

At Yaddo in 1967, for example, she met the writer John Marquand who, with the support of his wealthy wife Sue, would become Janet's major patron in the United States for the next decade. In 1968 and 1969 she shared holidays with the Marquands on an island that they rented in the Bahamas. On another occasion she stayed with them at Martha's Vineyard, playground of the rich and famous on the eastern seaboard of the United States. At MacDowell in 1969 she formed a close friendship with the Californian artist Bill Brown, whom she would describe as 'the chief experience of my life'. That friendship with Brown, and with his partner, fellow artist Paul Wonner, would persist over more than three decades. Through Brown, Frame met other writers such as May Sarton, Stephen Spender and Christopher Isherwood; and Isherwood's partner, Don Bachardy, drew a fine portrait of her in 1969. On almost all these visits to the United States and subsequent ones, Janet would spend part of her time staying with John Money in Baltimore, and she would also visit George Braziller and Carl Brandt in New York.

In July 1972, Frame surprised her Dunedin friends by abandoning the deep south for Whangaparaoa north of Auckland. The location of the Opoho house had become

141

Sue and John Marquand at Salt Cay in the Bahamas. This wealthy and generous couple became Janet's major patrons in the United States. JAMES MARQUAND

The MacDowell colony in New Hampshire was not established or funded as lavishly as Yaddo, but it provided another writing sanctuary for Janet in 1969. JANET FRAME

Janet takes a pause from work in her studio deep in the woods at MacDowell. Janet Frame

**Drawing of Janet
by Don Bachardy,
California, December
1969.**
ALEXANDER TURNBULL LIBRARY

Janet at MacDowell
with Bill Brown, the
artist she described
as 'the chief experience
of my life'.
JANET FRAME

With Paul Wonner,
Bill Brown's partner, at
Montecito, California.
JANET FRAME

Janet's bedroom and study in the basement of John Money's house in East Baltimore. Despite her anxieties about violence in the neighbourhood, this was to be her primary base in the United States over three decades.
JOHN MONEY

Janet and sexologist John Money on the stoop in front of his row house in Baltimore, March 1982.
JOHN MONEY

progressively more noisy. Whangaparaoa seemed quiet and tropical by contrast, and was less than an hour away from where Janet's sister June lived with her family. Janet continued to travel, however. In 1974 she won the Katherine Mansfield fellowship, which took her to Menton on the French-Italian border and allowed her to revisit friends in England and the United States.

In 1975, pursued by her old enemy, neighbourhood noise, she shifted house from Whangaparaoa to the Auckland suburb of Glenfield. And then, the following year, she began a series of moves that would take her to a succession of rural and provincial towns in the North Island over the next two decades: Stratford, where she lived in two properties in succession; Wanganui; Levin (again, two

The town of Menton on the French-Italian border. Because of its strong association with Katherine Mansfield, Janet spent seven months there on a writer's fellowship in 1974. ALEXANDER TURNBULL LIBRARY

Janet at Whangaparaoa
in 1974 with June, niece
Pamela and Pamela's
one-year-old daughter
Josie.
PAMELA GORDON

On her motorcycle
early in 1981.
On this occasion she
had made a 264 kilo-
metre round trip
between Wanganui
and her sister's home
in Levin.
JANET FRAME

Janet (right) with her friend Ruth Dallas represent New Zealand at the PEN Congress in Sydney in 1977. RUTH DALLAS

houses); Shannon; and Palmerston North (two houses). Some of these moves were precipitated by noise, and some by the wish to live near her sister and brother-in-law, who shifted almost as frequently as did Janet herself over these years.

A consequence of this degree of disruption to her writing life was that the rate of books written and published slowed. Janet produced only two more novels: *Living in the Maniototo* (1979) and *The Carpathians* (1988); and one more book of stories, *You Are Now Entering the Human Heart* (1983). Perhaps her most important books of the period were her three volumes of autobiography, *To the Is-Land* (1982), *An Angel at My Table* (1984), and *The Envoy from Mirror City* (1985). These told her version of the story of her life up to the time of her return to New Zealand from England in 1963. They and the Jane Campion feature film based on them, *An Angel at My Table* (1990), opened up for Janet a far wider readership than she had enjoyed previously – in New Zealand, Australia, the United States and Europe. They also resulted in all her work coming back into print, much of it in foreign language editions.

Her fame grew with the increasing popularity of and respect for her work. She won awards for her writing in New Zealand and the United States; and, later, in Italy and Chile. Her books were praised by fellow writers as varied as Patrick White, Doris Lessing and Michael Holroyd. She came to be spoken of as a contender for the Nobel Prize in Literature. And, after 1990, her work in print was generating sufficient income for her never to have to worry again about money.

There were other causes of anxiety in her life, however. In Palmerston North in the early 1990s she suffered a mild stroke. And, in 1992, she had an operation to remove a cancerous ovarian cyst. In the wake of the

OPPOSITE: **The four Janets on the set of Jane Campion's film *An Angel at My Table*, Auckland, 1989. Kerry Fox (right) went on to a successful international acting career. BRIDGET IKIN**

Janet at the International Festival of the Arts in Wellington in 1994, where her seventieth birthday was celebrated. Karl Stead, at left, is happy to be photographed. She is not and displays customary surprise and shock at being a target for the cultural paparazzi. MARTI FRIEDLANDER

By the 1990s Frame was frequently represented as an emblem of **New Zealand** literary culture. In this cartoon by Tom Scott she tackles a representative of the country's far more pervasive rugby culture.
Tom Scott

In one of Janet's rare public appearances she takes her place (front, second left) at a reunion of Otago University Burns fellows in 1998. Maori writer Witi Ihimaera (far left) described her as an elder of the tribe who gave her colleagues a sense of pride and security. Reg Graham

With her sister June, brother-in-law Wilson and her biographer, Janet explores Frame associations with Glenham in Southland, more than seventy years after the family lived there. REG GRAHAM

Janet with Pamela Gordon, who would eventually settle in the same Dunedin street three houses away from her aunt.
PAMELA GORDON

A last visit to the oldest and most loyal of her publishers, George Braziller, in 2000, the year her biography was published in the United States.
PAMELA GORDON

OPPSOITE: **Sibling survivors: Janet and June at St Clair Beach, Dunedin, 1999.**
REG GRAHAM

156

latter, she was informed that she probably had no more than six months to live. The cancer went into remission, however, and she survived. In 1995 Janet moved back to Auckland. Then, two years later, she followed her sister, brother-in-law and niece back to Dunedin, where she has remained, pronouncing herself in harmony with her ghosts there. She has had no new major work published since *The Carpathians* in 1988. The income from her backlist is such that she no longer needs to publish new writing to support herself.

The only recent new book with which she has been closely involved is her biography, *Wrestling with the Angel*, published in 2000. To assist the author, she gave up hundreds of hours to interviews, visiting old home places, and reading and checking draft chapters and proofs. She did not welcome the promotional attention given to her life in the wake of the publication of this volume, but she endured and survived it. She continues to write daily. Her fans still hope for the appearance of new work from Janet Frame – fiction, poetry or autobiography. Janet declines to say whether or not she will oblige them. They take heart and hope from the fact that she is still an active writer.

OPPOSITE: **The Janet Frame most beloved of her friends and family: vibrant, wickedly funny, full of mischief, an enjoyer and enhancer of life. Here she tap-dances on the bare boards of Frank Sargeson's former house in Takapuna, Auckland.**
MICHAEL KING

Great-niece Josie feeds the chooks at Janet's farmlet in Shannon in 1988. Janet looks on protectively.
PAMELA GORDON

BIBLIOGRAPHY: JANET FRAME'S BOOKS

The bulk of Janet Frame's published work is in print in English in New Zealand, the United Kingdom and the United States. In foreign language editions, her fiction and autobiographies are published in French, German, Norwegian, Swedish, Danish, Italian, Dutch, Polish, Spanish, Japanese, Hungarian and Chinese.

The following list provides the year of first publication only.

FICTION

The Lagoon and Other Stories, 1951 (1952)
Owls Do Cry, 1957
Faces in the Water, 1961
The Edge of the Alphabet, 1962
Snowman, Snowman: Fables and Fantasies, 1963
The Reservoir: Stories and Sketches, 1963
Scented Gardens for the Blind, 1963
The Adaptable Man, 1965
A State of Siege, 1966
The Rainbirds, 1968 (*Yellow Flowers in the Antipodean Room*, US edition, 1969)
Mona Minim and the Smell of the Sun, 1969
Intensive Care, 1970
Daughter Buffalo, 1972
Living in the Maniototo, 1979
You Are Now Entering the Human Heart, 1983
The Carpathians, 1988

POETRY

The Pocket Mirror, 1967

AUTOBIOGRAPHY

To the Is-Land, 1982
An Angel at my Table, 1984
The Envoy from Mirror City, 1985

BIBLIOGRAPHY: BOOKS ABOUT JANET FRAME

Alley, Elizabeth (ed.), *The Inward Sun, Celebrating the Life and Work of Janet Frame*, Daphne Brassell, 1994

Dalziel, Margaret, *Janet Frame*, Oxford University Press, 1980

Delbaere, Jeanne (ed.), *The Ring of Fire, Essays on Janet Frame*, Dangaroo Press, 1992

Evans, Patrick, *An Inward Sun, The Novels of Janet Frame*, New Zealand University Press/Price Milburn, 1971

Evans, Patrick, *Janet Frame*, Twayne, 1977

Ferrier, Carole (ed.), *The Janet Frame Reader*, The Women's Press, 1995

King, Michael, *Wrestling with the Angel, A Life of Janet Frame*, Viking, 2000

Leaver-Cooper, Sheila and Smith, Ian S., *Janet Frame's Kingdom by the Sea: Oamaru*, Lincoln University Press/Daphne Brassell, 1997

Mercer, Gina, *Janet Frame, Subversive Fictions*, Queensland University Press, 1994

Panny, Judith Dell, *I Have What I Gave, The Fiction of Janet Frame*, Daphne Brassell, 1992